A MIDDLE-AGED MUNROIST

A Middle-Aged Munroist

Peter Knight

The Pentland Press
Edinburgh – Cambridge – Durham – USA

First published in 1998 by
The Pentland Press Ltd
1 Hutton Close
South Church
Bishop Auckland
Durham

ISBN 1 85821-627 3

Typeset in Plantin
by Carnegie Publishing, Carnegie House, Chatsworth Road, Lancaster
Printed and bound by Antony Rowe Ltd, Chippenham

To Hazel –

the one who matters most of all

Contents

Illustrations and Photographs

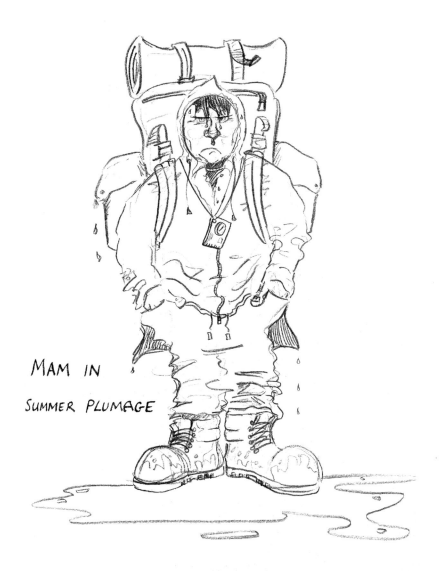

MAM IN

SUMMER PLUMAGE

Dramatis Personae

Hazel	My wife
We/us/our	Hazel and I/Hazel and me/Hazel's and my, or otherwise as made clear by the context
Philip, Andrew,	
Vicky and Sara	Our children
You/your	The general reader/reader's; an aspiring middle-aged munroist (mam/mam's)
Anna	Friend and neighbour in Edinburgh
Australian Tim	Philip's brother-in-law in Sydney
Dieter	One of Sara's then boyfriends
Dominic	Another of Sara's then boyfriends
Douglas and	
Patricia	Friends in Glen Urquhart
Fred	Friend in Edinburgh
George	Friend and Minister of Cluny Parish Church, Edinburgh
Gérard	Yet another of Sara's then boyfriends
Hugh and Sheila	Friends in Glen Lonan
James	Philip's son, our first grandchild
Jo	Our niece
Ken W.	Friend in Bearsden and Bartholomews' librarian
Nick and Greg	Our nephews in California
Oliver	Friend in Livingston
Philip R.	Ros's stepson, friend of our children
Richard	Friend in Steeple Aston
Ros	Friend in Melbourne
Rupert	Vicky's husband
Sarah and Lisa	Our niece and her friend in Melbourne
Tim	Our brother-in-law
Tony and Iris	Friends in Edinburgh

1

The Munros   The eponymous publication of the Scottish Mountaineering
               Club, second edition 1991, hereinafter referred to as M

together with numerous and various fellow climbers and walkers, landowners,
factors, farmers, fishermen, herdsmen, shepherds, policemen, water and elec-
tricity company employees, operators of chair-lifts, professional path repairers,
B&B keepers and hotel owners, as well as many strolling huntsmen, game-
keepers and stalkers, and last, but certainly not least, Cuillin Guides, to whom
my thanks are due for their strategic technical support when it was most
needed.

Particular thanks are also due to my honorary linguistic consultant and
proof-reader, Hal Stuart, who cares more about apostrophes than anyone else
I know. All pedantry and poor use of English I can now confidently blame
on him! Finally, a special accolade is awarded to Dominic Johnson for his
illustrations, each one of which captures the mood of the moment exactly.
He espoused the cause in so many ways.

CHAPTER I

Genesis

Ideas for this book first began to take real shape halfway up Beinn Alligin on a most beautiful day in the spring of 1994. It was to be my 163rd Munro. The day before had been diametrically atrocious and I was defeated by the Five Sisters, or rather, by the other four. As 'difficult, demanding women' I had described them, much to the amusement of a team of ladies descending Sgurr Mhor.

DIFFICULT, DEMANDING WOMEN

One meets the most interesting folk in the Scottish hills and mountains: like the young couple who carried their first-born infant son up Gleouraich, his first Munro, at nine weeks old; or James and Barbara, postgraduate Melburnians, on Bruach na Frithe, doing their first on Skye; or the Geordie father and son who had strolled – their word – up Sgurr na Banachdich without benefit of map or compass, whom I sent down before the weather changed for the worse – which it was about to – and who still managed to descend the wrong corrie, but fortunately made a soft landing. It is, perhaps, the greatest pleasure of being there. A few are taciturn, buried deep in their own thoughts, their own ideas of what it's all about, their own pain and joy. They carry clear personal 'DO NOT DISTURB' notices fore and aft and pass by with no communion, no exchange of news and views, loners in their chosen domain, and nothing wrong with that.

Most, however, are glad of a break, to share the experience, to trade food, weather forecasts, plans for the future, historic triumphs, even a dram. These exchanges are usually anonymous. It is incredibly easy in the hills to reveal and have revealed to one the most intimate and personal thoughts, knowing that they will be kept as secret as in the confessional, things that one wouldn't reveal to one's best friend. In many such conversations I have discussed with the willing listener my plan to climb all the Munros and their adjacent Tops for the first time over the age of fifty, and thereby graduate as a mam. In the event of such as the Inaccessible Pinnacle defeating me, I would ask for my ashes to be scattered there, thus becoming the posthumous munroist. The notion was probably never taken very seriously by either party to the discussion!

The exchange on Beinn Alligin was, however, different. We introduced ourselves. They were Jim and Ken from the West of Scotland. At first we didn't climb together but throughout the day our paths became inextricably linked. My idea captured their imagination. We had harmonious views on important matters such as the difficulty of bringing up children in this modern world, and the relative importance of Glasgow and Edinburgh in the overall scheme of things.

I had first seen them stopped some way ahead and on coming level found them busy with the mechanics of filling bottles from a waterfall. The first rounds of our conversation were routine and clearly laid bare the effects of their previous night's bevvying. I went on ahead but Jim was not far behind, going faster than me, and we reached the top of Tom na Gruagaich together. I speculated about Ken's general potential for finishing the job in hand; Jim was quite sanguine, however, and it became clear that they were frequent climbing companions. Sure enough, Ken duly appeared over the ridge, mumbling unspeakable thoughts about his general condition, and the trio were reunited.

I started ahead of them on the traverse to Sgurr Mhor but they passed me on the way to the summit, now clearly into their regular stride. We descended together, Jim – now known as Young Lochinvar – going over the Horns, and Ken and I taking the bypass.

From our exchanges the first thoughts of writing a book developed. If Jim or Ken ever read this, then thank you both for the initial inspiration. I hope you find it interesting and not completely libellous. I have not changed the names to protect the innocent!

That day ended in a way similar to many. Jim clearly wanted to maintain a fast pace while Ken and I were happy to amble home. Home was the car park near Inveralligin. I asked Jim to look out for Hazel, either walking towards us up the path by the Abhainn Coire Mhic Nobuil or in the car park itself.

Hazel is now quite used to being accosted by strange, in the sense of unfamiliar, men bearing usually good news about her husband's whereabouts, and I use this technique, if that word is appropriate, to inform her of my running later than expected –

a not infrequent occurrence – and of my general safe condition. She is there, of course, with a car full of goodies – food, drink, dry clothes, warmth, a sympathetic ear, and we gladly shared our cornucopia with my most engaging companions of the day.

The next day they were bound north of Loch Maree, whereas I had Liathach in view. What better mountain for May Day – if the weather held – which it did!

Torridon is my favourite area overall in Scotland. It is God's own country – a matter I shall return to later. My first visit had been some ten years before, and before the Munro bug had bitten. With young children I had been confined to low-level walks but the longish one to Kerrysdale through the Flowerdale Forest I had done alone. To any of you wanting to experience the essence of the beauty of Wester Ross without climbing Munros, I can thoroughly recommend it. But for those as yet inexperienced in such matters I should, perhaps, explain that there is no longer any forest. That and other such went years ago. This country is pure wilderness.

CHAPTER II

Exodus

I have always loved walking the hills and being in wild places, and I am equally happy being alone or in company. That statement will remain axiomatic for the time being – I will endeavour to explain and justify it later. Meantime, let's just say it's the way I'm made. If you are made similarly you should enjoy the book and perhaps be moved to put some of its ideas into practice yourselves. If not, well – I hope you will enjoy the book anyway!

On the whole I prefer to be on foot than to use any other form of transport. We live about a mile and a half from Edinburgh city centre and I would rather walk to and from town whatever the weather. In buildings with lifts I will normally choose to climb up and down a dozen or so floors rather than be carried. It's also a low-risk strategy, for staircases do not break down.

We came to Edinburgh from the South and lived in several of its suburbs until finally settling in Morningside over twenty years ago. Each new location was very fully explored on foot, as well as the City itself. Edinburgh has a three-dimensional topography and this is best discovered as a pedestrian. For example, our then contemporary map showed Johnston Terrace as intersecting King's Stables Road rather than flying over it, and a motorist planning a journey based upon such an error would only recover his position after some delay. To those on foot, however, there is no problem, as the two levels are linked by a fine sandstone staircase.

As incomers, viewing Edinburgh like a blank canvas, as it were, we could research and discover it impartially, with none of the deep-seated preconceptions of the native. It took about three years, I recall, to become really familiar with the geography. The journeys from this to that suburb were always the most difficult to work out. This is particularly true on the west side of the City where the inheritance of live and disused railway lines together with the Union Canal created well-defined nodes through which motor transport is possible but not elsewhere, and with a different set of nodes accessible to cyclists and pedestrians.

At that time I evolved a simple theory which worked very well. The shortest journey time by car between any two points in Edinburgh was that which crossed the fewest traffic lights. This was valid at any time of the day or night, in and out of rush hours. I'm not sure if it is still so. There has been a proliferation of lights over the period and, anyway, we are the same as natives now, ploughing our own well-worn furrows. I do still notice, however, when being driven about the City by a real native, that he will use the obvious routes with which he grew up and not the usually faster but possibly more obscure ones which we may have worked out for ourselves, based on our advantage – if, indeed, it was such – of having lived in more different places in the City than most.

This is still a good game to play, but it is now much more complicated than it was in those seemingly innocent days. For example, there are half a dozen quite distinct routes from Morningside to Leith, ranging through Holyrood Park at one extreme to Ravelston at the other. None is self-evidently better than any other, and certainly not Morningside Road/Leith Walk. Any one could be faster or more convenient than any other, depending on time of day, time of year, in and out of the

Festival, day of week, and whether the City centre is occupied with a visiting cycle race, miners' gala or royal visit. With such thoughts I amuse myself in traffic jams …

Apart from interest in the surrounding geography of a new abode, my youth had equipped me with three skills which are essential for the aspiring mam or, indeed, munroist in general. The first was map-reading, learnt through the school cadet force. We did theory in the classroom and went out into the fells of northern England or the mountains of north and central Wales for the practical. The teaching was repetitive but thorough. We used the old war department OS 1″, overprinted with the military's own grid system in violent purple. I came to love maps as great technical achievements if not works of art, and the 1″ became a definitive standard. All the conventional signs had to be committed to memory, we were required to work out using the shape of the contour lines whether point A could be seen from point B and, in the field, we were drilled in distance judging in various qualities of light, looking up or down, into the sun or away from it and, above all, across unfathomable gaps in the terrain. We could tell a church with a spire from a church with a tower from a church with neither – but not its denomination! These basic skills I now cherish. They never really leave you in spite of, in my case, a long period of disuse. You must acquire them if you aspire to make a success of the Scottish or any other hills.

The second was how to use a compass and, in conjunction with the first, how to set a map so that it can be followed in near-zero visibility. It is essential in fog or, indeed, any other mountain weather conditions to be able to point to your map and say 'I am there' with total conviction. If you can't then you are lost. If you are lost you are in danger. The problem is not insoluble. However, following a compass bearing without knowing exactly from where you are starting is at best uncomfortable, and at worst life-threatening. If, of course, you are born and

Routes difficult by Perthshire standards – Coire Lagan from top to bottom.

bred in the hills and know your hinterland intimately – every rock and tussock – you can navigate simply by knowing the ways of the winds. But then you will be one who climbs mountains only when he needs to!

The third was basic rock-climbing with ropes. There are easy and difficult routes up all the Munros, and I am expecting my aspiring mams on the whole to select the easier ones. However, these are relative terms. The easy routes in Skye are exceedingly difficult by Perthshire standards. Apart from the Inaccessible Pinnacle, I have done all my Scottish climbing without ropes for, as you will see, I prefer to travel light, but one is certainly helped by having the basic scrambling techniques, if only to judge objectively what can and shouldn't be attempted.

Now is the time to make it categorically clear that it is not the purpose of this book to impart basic climbing technique. There are many excellent volumes, far better than I could ever write, which do this and towards which I would direct the less experienced among you. Apart from the above three skills, which are essentially practical things which must be perfected out there in the mountains in all varieties of conditions, you should also be versed in most of the following: reading the weather, basic survival, basic first aid for yourself and others, recognizing and responding to the symptoms of hypothermia and dehydration, understanding the various shooting and stalking seasons and what may and may not be done therein, the unique problems and techniques of winter excursions and, perhaps above all, how to practise minimal trace climbing, that is, to leave the wilderness just as you found it.

With increasing experience you will also learn how to follow a vestigial path through bog and snow with the facility of an American Indian, how best to deal with landowners and other country interests, how to distinguish between a sheep and a deer trail, and both from a stalker's or climber's path (and the importance of knowing the distinction), and all four from a dried out quartzite gravel bed which goes nowhere in particular. You will learn those flora which presage boggy ground – for you'll need to know your morass from your moraine – and come, thereby, to a great love of small, colourful alpine plants clinging tenaciously to their precarious mountain existence. You will also need to develop a Franciscan love of midges, clegs, flies, other blood-sucking winged beasties, and uncontrolled dogs which will bound up and thrust their dripping noses straight into your crutch. You will be able to unfold a map in high speed, wind-driven horizontal sleet, getting from it accurately the information you want in the shortest possible time, and then fold it up again.

I hope all this isn't putting you off, but it would be totally irresponsible of me to suggest that hill-walking was no harder than going on a family picnic. There is risk, of course, in walking to post a letter. The risk in the hills is of a totally different order, but should never be compounded by ignorance or incompetence.

If you will confine your walking to the summer months of June, July, and the first half of August; if you will only go out in fine weather in the clearest visibility; if you will turn back at the first spot of rain (and on Beinn Narnain I met one who habitually did); if you will never plant your dainty footprint in a snowfield; if you will climb only by the safest and most well-worn tracks; if you will never put yourself on a gradient of more than 20°; if you will always plan to be down again by four in the afternoon, then you might get by without most of these skills and this knowledge. But your experience will be diminished and you will miss much of the joy.

Every winter we lose fifteen to twenty climbers in the Scottish mountains. I grieve for them and their loved ones. They are not novices. These are experienced folk, well equipped, who know what they are doing. They compute the percentages but lose. A sudden change of weather, sprained ankle, unexpected fall, a misreading of the map or compass, a miscalculation of the time required, the loss or failure of a vital piece of equipment, some other gross piece of bad luck – who knows? This is life and death. That, of course, is partly why we do it. The challenge is overwhelming and irresistible.

So, be warned – be properly equipped, know what you are about and are taking on, and derive the deepest and most uplifting satisfaction from it. Of course, all these skills and techniques will feature later in the story, if only to underpin its narrative. But I make the point again – this book is not written as an instruction manual. If you are inexperienced, do something about it first!

Nor is it intended to offer detailed routes except, as above, to illustrate particular points by example or to carry the story along. Use M for that; every aspiring mam should have one. It is succinct, very well written and, when used in conjunction with the appropriate map, will offer you an unambiguous way up and down with its various snags and potential dangers fully exposed. However, there are two things I would say about M, not as criticism, but simply so that you will know. The first is that it is somewhat conservative – which I'll illustrate later – the second is that, on the whole, and except for such obvious collections as the various Sisters, it tends to treat the Munros singly. One thing I will be doing is to consider and recommend combinations of hills which I have done and which, at first sight, may not seem obvious. Also, M does not treat the Tops fully, tending to cover them as access routes or incidental to the main climb. Tops, however, are by no means a pushover. Have you tried Meall Dearg on Liathach? Nor are Sgurr Dubh and Meall Mor just given away. You could also investigate the extremities of An Teallach without going over the Munros as an interesting, worthwhile and unconventional assignment.

It probably follows from the above that my plan is not to mention every Munro and Top by name. I shall deal individually with only those that best serve to illustrate some particular point, or those during the course of climbing which there was something of special interest or amusement to relate. If I haven't referred to your own particular favourite, therefore, it does not necessarily follow that I love it any less than you do.

So, what is this book about? First I should define my mam, for you are my blood brother. You are close to my heart. I understand you. You and I are one. We have special needs and aspirations which are not fully addressed by the other books. That, basically, is why I have written this one. Mams:

❋ Are fit over-forties who want to stay fit, or unfit over-forties who want to become fit.

❋ Have the ever-undiminished will to sustain a concerted campaign over a period of five years or more without becoming downhearted or disillusioned.

❋ Are required to juggle their thrust towards the hills with business, work and family commitments so that none of these is thereby undermined or appears to suffer, including the maintenance of the garden, the lawn especially.

❋ Are adept at spending a Saturday afternoon enthralled by a school play, concert, prize-giving or sports day without giving anybody – most of all junior dramatist, musician, prize-winner or athlete – the slightest hint as to where they would rather be.

❋ Prefer to spend nights in their own beds, failing which, in some comfortable hostelry, rather than a tent, bothy or bivvy bag.

❋ Like to bath or shower in hot water and using soap at the end of each day.

❋ Would rather start a consecutive climbing day with dry clothes, and boots in particular.

❋ Climb as much as is physically possible in one day, as they realize that their time is limited, that is, some twenty years shorter than that available to the lithe, bronzed thing that flashed past on that gruelling final pull to the summit.

✻ Climb as much as is physically possible in one day in order to get the maximum value for money from the cost of the outward and return journeys.

✻ Become expert in climbing myopically, as their glasses, when steamed, watered or iced up, slide precipitously down their noses, far enough to be of no effective use. (Mine were once nearly lost to a yawning chasm on An Teallach. Fortunately they came to rest on an accessible, prominent rock).

✻ Have recalcitrant teenage offspring for whom a hard day in the mountains could just work wonders.

✻ Dream about long nights in the Andean Chain or on Kilimanjaro when the time comes that they can afford to turn the dream into the reality, for this ultimately is why they want to keep so fit for so long ...

Although not intended in its original conception, the extent to which the book was tending towards autobiography became clear during its early proof-reads. I take comfort from the fact that Trollope was of the view that 'The man of letters is, in truth, ever writing his own biography. What there is in his mind is being declared to the world at large by himself.' Not that I would claim to be taken seriously as a man of letters. However, the preponderance of I's and me's became disturbing. I will justify them for the fact that they lend immediacy and vigour to the story, and have abandoned any well-meant attempt to replace them with self-effacing circumlocutions.

When we first came to Scotland I had, of course, heard of the Munros, but only in a very generalized way. I was under the impression that anything over 3,000′ came within the definition, without thinking about it at all deeply. I certainly had no plan to climb them in any concerted way, but simply to venture forth into the hills as and when the opportunity arose, to enjoy what I had always enjoyed.

It is part of the natural life cycle that, after marriage and while learning and exercising basic parentcraft, the things of one's youth must be placed to the side while other responsibilities take priority. Thus it was not until after several years, when Philip and Andrew were into their teens and themselves keen to sample the great outdoors, that I ventured forth once again, this time into the delightful rolling border hills to the south. Then came the most unexpected, uncalled for, utterly tiresome and quite frightening discovery. I suffered from acrophobia.

How this could be I have never understood, given my own youthful and carefree exposure to some quite severe climbs. I who had led whole parties of schoolkids along Striding Edge without blinking and had stridden the ramparts of the Taigetos seven days after a Greek appendicectomy was now here on the technically undemanding ridges of Lochcraig Head and couldn't bear to look down into Loch Skeen 800' below.

Overcoming it was a deliberate and painstaking process requiring patience, determination and a degree of wilfulness, and I have only really mentioned this in order to encourage those among you who feel that you haven't a good head for heights. Experiment in places which present no threat; take a sympathetic friend – hand to hold, even; explore what is possible and work on it. Over time I feel sure that you will make progress. Even now I can operate more effectively on an exposed knife-edge ridge in swirling mist rather than with a clear view when the outcome of a fall would be brought literally into focus.

These are strange matters which I don't comprehend at all and I will have cause to return to them later in the story. For the moment it will be sufficient to record that Ben Cruachan became my phobia cracker, from easy slope in the beginning to the great ridge walk in final conquest. After the Munros I shall do it again – all seven peaks in a oner – as a triumphant lap of honour, saved for a fine summer's day. It is my all-time favourite mountain of any I know, and for a variety of reasons.

One of our much-loved holiday places when the children were young was in Glen Lonan at Hugh and Sheila's magnificent Lorimer mansion. This we attended over several years in the most pleasant company of many and varied family friends and their offspring. It was thus that Ben Cruachan or, more precisely, Stob Dearg became home territory, and Hugh my great educator as to its possibilities. Before continuing that train of thought, however, I should like to say a few words about Callander.

These were the days before the M9 to Stirling had been completed. To reach Callander ahead of the first requested pit stop was a major performance indicator. Thus the town became our mythical crock of gold – hang on till then and the rewards would be bountiful. It's a super wee place. We have tried every hostelry from the Myrtle Inn in the east to the Lade Inn at Kilmahog, and most in between. As the children grew and their demands changed and became more sophisticated so we graduated from chips and tomato sauce with everything to those taverns offering discos, pool tables and arcade machines. No family need go hungry or thirsty in Callander. All pockets and tastes are fully catered for.

Now, of course, with the children away, a quieter approach is possible. Consider the side trip to the Bracklinn Falls for your elderly folk or others no longer capable of Munros. This half-mile, almost level walk from the car park is well worth doing, and can be covered in what the books used to describe as stout walking shoes. The water is the outflow from the corries and glacial trenches of Stuc a' Chroin and Beinn Each and in the spring is spectacular.

On the subject of easier walks I can also recommend the railway path which runs to the west of Loch Lubnaig. It is, by definition, almost flat and offers a no-sweat alternative, car-free

entry into that beautiful place. The old track bed is now paved
and offers facilities both to walkers and cyclists. Higher up the
strath heading north the former Stirling to Crianlarich railway
climbed from Lochearnhead to the top of Glen Ogle. This was
a superb piece of Victorian railway engineering and includes,
still intact, the only stone viaduct in the world, I believe, to
have been built parallel with the valley floor rather than across
it.

One of my future plans – after the Munros! – is to walk the
old track bed in both directions from the top as far as is possible.
The integrity of the route is not preserved, however, as newer
road building and widening have claimed some of the space.
This could be more difficult to do, therefore, than it might
otherwise have been. Old railway embankments leading to demolished bridges are quickly colonized by impenetrable
undergrowth and one is forever descending and regaining the
track bed. Perhaps I will then write the retired mams' guide to
walking disused railway lines.

It was near Callander that the car broke down when I was
taking Tim for an excursion into the Crianlarich Hills, Cruach
Ardrain in particular, and as much of the rest as we could
reasonably manage in a day. Tim, used to long walks, was
incredibly fit – much more so than me. The approach was to
be along Loch Voil and would take in the elegant and gracefully
sculpted profile of Stob Binnein from Balquhidder, always assuming that the clouds would part for long enough for it to be
profiled.

But it was the water pump that stopped us, just before the
Pass of Leny. The local police were pleasant and helpful, and
it was only an hour or so before the car had been removed to
its repair site and we were kindly driven back to the Stank by
the garage owner, who reasonably expected to complete the
repair by sundown and had suggested Ben Ledi as a not too
bad alternative to our planned climb.

Tim, however, wanted Munros, so I offered him Stuc a' Chroin. We walked the three miles along the A84 to join the track over to Glen Ample, and I vow to this day that that part of it is the most dangerous walk I have ever attempted in the Highlands. It was a relief to get off the main road and into the glen, well away from the traffic. The climb from the south-west was otherwise straightforward and we returned via the south-bound tourist route to Callander.

I had tried Stuc a' Chroin a year or so earlier with Sara, using the same route. When we had reached the Bealach nan Cabar and she could see from there how much yet remained to be done, she decided that enough was enough. Her experience to date had been confined to the Pentlands – this was to be the first Munro. The weather was horrible and I couldn't really blame her. There was no point in forcing the pace – that would simply provoke alienation from the joys which would eventually come her way. She wanted me to go on alone and collect her on the way back but that wasn't on. We returned together, defeated.

Callander is the one town which ought to proclaim itself 'Gateway to the Highlands' but doesn't. It truly is, though, both physically and metaphorically. The portal of the Pass of Leny opens onto a magnificent and majestic scene complete with the romance and mystery of Rob Roy country beyond, as if separated by a veil from the real world to the east. I'm told that somebody wanted to organize a pop festival up there in a field at Strathyre, blasting that so tranquil setting with gigawatts and decibels of the most horrendous kind. How can we be so barbarous? Fortunately it has not happened yet. Instead we suffer the ugliness of the caravans strewn about the same meadow.

There is a truth about Callander which I find both fascinating and sobering. Given a clear run, which is usually possible early in the morning at any time of the year, I can drive like a bat out of hell or like the aged grandpa that I am about to become, and it always takes exactly fifty-five minutes from home. Is there some as yet unexplained dimension of the theory of relativity at work behind that veil over the Falls of Leny which controls these matters? Who knows?

While discussing Callander and before returning to Hugh and Ben Cruachan, a word or two about Ben Ledi. This is, in all respects, a magnificent mountain. It is huge. My first ever sight of it was from Blackford Hill in Edinburgh on a clear day, some fifty miles distant. In those days of ignorance I had thought it was Ben More, such was its great size, and the direction was right. My apologies to all those visitors to Edinburgh who now think that Ben Ledi is Ben More!

On a clear day you can see it from the Glasgow train between Linlithgow and Falkirk High, in the company of Stuc a' Chroin and Ben Vorlich, but it looks much more massive and taller than both of those. Thus the myth of its being Ben More lingered on. Yet it does not quite make Munro status. On a very clear day you can, in fact, see Ben More behind, the first vision of which drove me back to the maps and to the beginning of the end of my long-standing fallacy.

On the approach to Callander from Stirling it is the sales graph mountain. A company launches a new product into the market place which is an immediate success and the monthly sales figures quickly and uniformly grow to a peak. It is a fashion item, however, and the public soon tires. The graph falls for a couple of months. Management, recognizing the trend, repackage the product and spend heavily on a TV advertising campaign. The downward trend is halted, but sales never regain their initial impetus and stay level for the next six months. Finally, a competitor introduces a better product at half the price and sales fall away out of sight.

Ben Ledi is always a surprise. Every time you see him from the summits of adjacent mountains, and many far away, you are surprised at his disposition. Here, from another angle, a different profile, there, the sales graph again, but always impressive, always massive. What's that hill over there – there are no Munros in that direction? It's Ben Ledi, of course, fooling us all, having the last laugh. Give him a day of your time – you'll be well rewarded.

Andrew had voted to do the climb from the Loch Venachar side, going straight up the sales graph and avoiding the tourist trail from the Stank. In terms of the weather it became our definitive and archetypal Highland walk. Nothing special to start with; couldn't see the top; however, at least it wasn't raining; hope springs eternal ...

Halfway up we got the first drenching of the day. By the top we had dried out in the wind. The encircling cloud ensured that there was no view. Continuing north along the graph we got the second soaking. Descending east to Loch Lubnaig we had once again dried out. When I return now from a climb and answer Andrew's question 'How was it?' with 'Typical Highland day', he knows exactly what I mean!

On that occasion we rehydrated at the Lade Inn having returned via the railway track. I discovered there that Andrew didn't like draught Guinness so I was able to have two pints to myself and let him drive home. It is always the case that the worst conceivable day out in the hills will contain something to make it memorable, and this one was no exception.

And so, back to Hugh of Taynuilt. He is the man who was motoring home up Strath Fillan when the driver of the 2CV in front discarded a used fag packet from his car window. Hugh was incensed and duly retrieved the offending article, following the fellow halfway across Rannoch Moor before he could return the litter to its owner. 'Kindly take your rubbish home with you lest you destroy that which you have come to marvel at' might be a suitable paraphrase of the opening bid! The fellow was duly mortified. All this happened many years ago. Doing the same today would, no doubt, put Hugh's very life at risk. Hugh is a Scottish gentleman of the best type – quiet, forthright, thinks deeply about the things which really matter, excellent company, a good raconteur, pours a straight dram and even possessing a degree of wisdom. I wish there were more like him.

That last paragraph was written over a year before Friday, 1 September 1995, the date of Hugh's death from a heart attack at an age far too young. I am happy to leave it unaltered as a tribute to a fine man and good friend of whom we shall retain many happy and lasting memories.

By this time of life, then, I had returned to the hills, had more or less overcome the fear of heights, had ventured forth in no particularly systematic way, had climbed Ben Nevis in summer by the tourist route with Philip R. and our boys, had about twenty-five Munros to my credit (or so I thought) and had climbed Ben Cruachan many times in a variety of ways and with a variety of companions, young and old, but still had not really focused on the notion of climbing them all systematically.

The catalyst for that was the appearance of M as a Christmas present from Philip and a map of Munros and Tops to stick pins in from Sara, almost as if the pair of them were conspiring to make it happen. Around twenty-five 'Munros' were swiftly reduced to half a dozen or fewer, as ineligible bumps which did not pass the M test or didn't quite make the necessary height were at a stroke eliminated from my burgeoning total. It now only needed Andrew's enthusiasm to set us on the long slippery slope, if that is a suitable metaphor for that to which we were about to commit ourselves. M told us that there were 277 Munros. By the time we had finished, however, the Scottish Mountaineering Club, which adjudicates these matters, had deleted one and added eight. Thus, as you will see, our final achievement was 284.

We set a rough target of fifty a year for five years with a final mopping up in year six. How disrespectful to our beloved scenery to analyse it thus! An average of one a week seemed daunting. How would we find the time? All answers will be duly revealed. We also agreed to include all the Tops, taking the 1990 revision of Munro's Tables – a fiftieth birthday present from Tony and Iris and, no doubt, also part of the conspiracy – as our definitive standard. Whether to approve or not of such tables, or their revision, is a subject outside the scope of this book and upon which most climbers with whom I have discussed it have their own well-considered views. It was important, however, to have well-set 'goalposts' which would not be moved. Thus Foinaven – which was being suggested for Munro status at the time of writing and of which there is a splendid view from the top of Ben Hope will be climbed for love and not as part of this campaign. And whether you include the Tops within your scope is entirely your own decision. Some do, some don't. Some, for completeness, take in the deleted Tops also.

I do detest the term 'Munro-bagging' and its derivatives. By concentrating purely on collecting scalps, on counting numbers, on pins in maps, it surely misses totally the point of such a venture, and this, I hope, will become clear in the following pages, at least as far as my own humble efforts are concerned. Perhaps most offensive is the implied notion of haste, of rushing round oblivious to the full delights of being in the wilderness. Nobody I know who walks the Scottish hills sees his ambition simply in terms of a headcount, and I am surprised that the term has been given such widespread currency. I shall not be using it again.

Not quite a Munro – Foinaven from the summit of Ben Hope

CHAPTER III

Numbers

I regard the planning of an excursion into the hills as a major exercise of fundamental importance. This is not to say that an opportunist thrust up some unknown glen or ridge as an antidote to a hot, steamy car journey is not occasionally a necessary piece of summer escapism, but to recognize that proper planning is required to get the best value for the time committed, and to give the best possible chance of a safe return.

In fact the planning is a most enjoyable exercise in its own right. The spending of our long dark evenings surrounded by a pile of maps, M and other reference sources, and sustained by a large dram, is one of the great pleasures of an Edinburgh winter.

LONG DARK EVENINGS SURROUNDED BY A PILE OF MAPS

Those of you familiar with the application of planning to business decision-making will see the obvious parallels between this and the preparation for a climb. The structural context is not so different, really. Here are its principal components.

Setting Objectives

This will start with a simple desire to address a particular set of Munros and Tops. It will be refined into a final, detailed route, giving start time, finish time and the sequence in which the peaks will be attempted. This will be the end product of a process of refinement as alternatives are considered and rejected. Methods of access and return will be included, together with all transport arrangements.

Commanding the Resources

Firstly, personal. You will have used your knowledge of your own capabilities to make a reasonable assessment of what's possible. But what about others – your climbing companions, or those upon whom you will be relying for the successful execution of your plan?

Secondly, equipment. What will you take? How much will you carry up the mountain? What are the options? If the weather at the start remains fine and hot will you leave your fleece in the car, or should you forgo the reduction in weight and bulk as an insurance against a possible change higher up?

Consideration of Alternatives

Whether the weather is a factor in any final night before (or even that morning) change of plan I'll leave to you. If it is, then each plan will need to have been equally well rehearsed, and the alternative not something hastily cobbled together on the outward journey. Fall-back positions should be fully worked out so that, if you need to come down before the planned finish, you won't be taken unawares.

Risk factors

This aspect of planning could be the most important for, in the extreme, you are putting your own life on the line. It is not possible to deal with risk comprehensively, but here are some components to be considered, which I have classified as major and minor:

Major

* The difficulty of the mountain itself and the route chosen. For Scotland this is well enough documented. The degree of exposure, the technical demands, the remoteness of the location and the likelihood of recovery are all relevant factors.

* The weather, including available daylight, which can add its own dimension to risk analysis.

* Yourself, your physical and mental state, your strength of character, your ability to cope with adversity and your performance under pressure.

* The same applied to your climbing companions.

* Your clothing and equipment, its sufficiency and practicality.

* The likelihood of a fall which, to a great extent, is heavily dependent on all the above.

* Loss of equipment.

Minor

❊ The state of your car and its petrol tank; transport arrangements generally.

❊ Landowners' barriers to access.

❊ Obstacles to progress such as rivers in spate, damaged crossings, blocked or overgrown paths.

❊ That you may need to truncate your journey and, therefore, return by an unplanned route, for it is not possible to plan in detail for every eventuality.

❊ Inaccuracies in the map.

When all this is weighed in the balance you must judge whether you will take the risk. You want to go. You will, therefore, reduce as far as possible all adverse factors, particularly the major ones. Are your boots looking worn – would they fail a boot MOT (and I would strongly suggest that 2mm of tread is not sufficient!)? If yes, buy some more. Is there a member in your planned party who comes by reputation but of whom you have no personal experience? How about the Buachaille as an alternative to the Aonach Eagach? Is the forecast such that compass navigation will be mandatory? How about Meall Chuaich rather than Sgor Gaoith? Are there youngsters in the party? What additional risk factors will thereby be in attendance?

I am risk-averse in the hills. I want to live!! I will not, for example, test the northern corries of Ben Nevis or venture far beyond the lip of the Lost Valley in winter or early spring, for there are risks here which I cannot control, nor can I reasonably estimate the likelihood of the event occurring. This is not cowardly, just practical, and operating well within the confines of one's own knowledge. Doing these things adds nothing to the quality of my experience, for I can get winter exposure much more safely (relatively speaking) elsewhere. If you do them, then you will have made your own risk assessment and found it acceptable. This will take into account your other responsibilities for family and business, for example. None of us is more right or wrong than the other. The only sin is to do such things foolhardily, with no understanding of, or care for, the dangers involved, not least to those who might come looking for you. Plan safely!

Execution

Assemble everything you need to take the night before. Put it somewhere where it won't be moved, borrowed or tidied away by other members of the family. Establish a routine so that, at that tired, fractious time of the morning, the whole thing will run like clockwork. If you are relying on others to furnish equipment, food, drink or transport then you are the manager and any shortcomings must be laid at your door. Take personal responsibility for an accurate watch, compass and maps.

If you are collecting climbing colleagues early in the morning then ensure they know exactly when they are to be ready – particularly the younger generation, who are not good in this department – and what they must bring with them. Consider housing them under your roof the night before so that you can administer a personal alarm call in parallel with preparing the early morning brew.

Check that everything you have put out is duly loaded into the car, particularly where other willing pairs of hands are helping.

And if you are driving, especially to the West, then park your car facing east to give it as much protection as possible from prevailing storms – or west if yours is one of those with the engine at the back!

Finally, you must leave those at home with a well-prepared routine to be brought into play if you don't return:

✳ Document your route and objectives, including alternatives. Say where you will park the car. Some leave this information behind the windscreen, and I wouldn't argue strongly against this except to say that, in our modern world, it may be as well not to advertise to a potential thief or vandal how much time is available for whatever he may have in mind.

✳ Give the latest time you expect to be back.

✳ Agree a time, say, three hours beyond this, after which an alert will be sounded.

✳ Agree the nature of this alert.

✳ Phone home before the three-hour deadline has expired if you are safe but simply running late.

✳ Remember that yuppiphones don't always work in the mountains and, where they do, the connection can be tenuous and intermittent. Therefore, learn where the public telephones are on the routes you use. Have the necessary coins available. In emergencies seek local help.

✳ If you are being met at a different finishing point then most of the above still applies, without your attendant being able to seek comfort in the thought that if you are late then you have most likely been held up in traffic. Also, phoning home may not be possible.

✳ Therefore, pay special attention to accurate timing and, if there is a straightforward walking route, encourage your escort to come and meet you.

✳ Use other walkers to carry news of your well-being, or otherwise.

✳ And, above all, ensure that the rendezvous is unambiguously understood, particularly if neither of you has been there before.

Planning can also be honed by the application of competent local wisdom, which is always worth tapping into when the day finally arrives. You may even find yourself staying close to a member of the local mountain rescue team, which must surely be a cause for comfort even although you will not, of course, ever need to have its services called upon on your behalf! An up-to-date weather commentary, an account of nearby river conditions and crossings, the advisability of a route you would like to try but perhaps are unsure of can all be explored for the small price of asking a few simple questions of the right people. Too little knowledge is a dangerous thing.

Planning is an iterative process. A winter evening's dream may not be put into practice until months, even years, later. By then your whole perception may have changed and your experience and willingness to test yourself further will have developed. Plan bravely – how about approaching A' Mhaighdean and Ruadh Stac Mor by boat across Loch Maree? There's nothing quite like a direct assault!

And now, to the fascinating subject of maps.

A map is a more or less accurate two-dimensional topographical model of a three-dimensional world. As such, it must be carefully researched before you can draw valid conclusions about that world which it is representing, and about which you may have no other source of information.

It took me a long time to become fully adapted to the OS 1:50,000 after being weaned onto the 1″ and I still prefer the copperplate, aesthetically pleasing look of the latter, with its fine detail which speaks with such clarity. However, progress is progress, and one cannot but admire the much more accurate presentation of contouring in the former – a very essential improvement for those of our persuasion. I assume that, as the newer technology improves, we shall eventually get a 1:50,000 with the quality of the 1″. What is interesting is to compare the old with the new. Accounting for differences is an intriguing and educational exercise.

Some of the major ones can be laid at the door of forestry activities, due to which there tend to be many more bulldozed tracks than are shown. These need care in interpretation as it is an easy trap for the unwitting to assume that the path they are on is the one on the map. Dense forests present challenges similar to those of fog. Use your compass if necessary. Forestry-induced change can be profound. Have a look at the rape of the northern corries of Beinn a' Bheithir as an example of what can be done under the influence of unbridled greed. The description of this superb mountain in M has been well and truly overtaken.

Some climbers swear by the 1:25,000, of which there are three in the 'Outdoor Leisure' series of interest to us – covering The Cairngorms, Glen Nevis, Torridon and Skye – as well as the regular edition covering the whole UK. I will not be dogmatic about this, but I find the larger scale ideal for planning – especially when used in conjunction with the 1:50,000 (accounting for differences again) – while using the smaller in the field. However, the larger scale Torridon map is particularly useful for Beinn Eighe which otherwise straddles two sheets, with three of its Tops inconveniently lying exactly on the border.

I have found in practice that, with constant use, there develops such a familiarity with the map that estimation of position and distance travelled comes without there having to be an intermediate process of survey or calculation. This facility is particularly useful in conditions of poor visibility, once you have the confidence to rely on it. In a sense, the map itself becomes the ground covered.

I first used the 1:25,000 in the Cairngorms and managed to start up the wrong ridge. It was the intimate familiarity that was missing. Logic says that a 1km square is a 1km square; only its size has changed. Real life defied the logic. Also, on that occasion, I should have put more time into the navigation than chatting to my most interesting companion of the day.

There is no doubt that the additional detail is welcomed by many. I do find, however, that the clutter of contour lines with rock features is not always easy to decipher, and the slight simplification of the smaller scale is a workable and acceptable approximation.

There are several formulae which will help you to work out how long your journey will take, some of them positively rococo in structure. My middle aged brain can only cope with simple things and I will now introduce you to some of the benefits of my findings.

The relationship between distance, time and gradient is at the heart of all this. If you are walking up a 45° slope then you are travelling nearly 50% further than will be read from the map as horizontal distance (remember Pythagoras from distant Geometry lessons?). Over a particular route the combined effect of all these ups and downs as well as the multitudinous horizontal zigs and zags is difficult, if not impossible, to calculate, partly because our mountains are not so neatly built as to be all of this or that gradient. Some are wee bauchles, some muckle great tents and others have shapes which defy metaphor in either Scots or English.

M describes Stob Ban – the easternmost of the Grey Corries – as 'a remote peak, far distant from any main road and hidden behind its higher neighbours'. However, there is a splendid view of her from the road along the north bank of Loch Laggan over several miles. From here she appears to be holding hands with her elder brothers, Stob a' Choire Mheadhoin and Stob Choire Claurigh. The descent to the bealach between Stob Ban and Stob Choire Claurigh is 45° over most of the distance. When you climb her, up or down, you will know what 45° feels like. 'Steep', you will say.

Now look at Stob Ban on OS 41. Normally there are four thin brown contour lines (each 10m vertically distant from its neighbour) between adjacent thick ones (representing a vertical difference of 50m). On the descent we are describing there are only two thin contour lines between adjacent thick ones – there isn't enough space to show more.

My second example is An Stuc, a Ben Lawers Top at the time, but now upgraded to full Munro status and, therefore, to be taken even more seriously. You can see this one from the Bealach Breabag between Ben Alder and Sron Coire na h-Iolaire. The left hand (north-east) ridge, connecting An Stuc to Meall Garbh, is 60° over most of its length. When you do climb it, you may decide that you wouldn't want to be on anything steeper.

Have a look at the contours of this ridge on OS 51. There is just one thin line squeezed in between adjacent thick ones.

Now if you are satisfied with following documented routes where the dangers are fully discussed by the authors recommending them then all this is, perhaps, of passing interest only. If, however, you want to pioneer your own way then it becomes much more important. In short, you need to read between the contour lines.

If there are just two thin lines between adjacent thick ones then you will be in for quite a pull (or drop). If rock features are shown there may be steep crags to be worked round. In your journey planning consider how best to do this. If there is just one thin line then you are probably operating at the limit of hill-walking as opposed to climbing. Take care. Have an alternative route planned so that, on the day, you can divert to it if the terrain you find makes this seem prudent. If there are no thin contour lines at all then keep off! Use due discretion when considering all this. The number of fine lines between adjacent thick ones is often a matter of the curvature of the contour itself – tighter round a thin Sron, for example – and the existence of other features like rock bands or scree which the cartographer has wished to show. As an absolute indicator, take the separation of thick contours as definitive.

One of the major limitations of the 1:50,000 series is that it says little about the nature of the terrain. That which is possible on a dry grass slope will be purgatorial over boulders, wearisome in waist-high ferns and difficult and time consuming on mobile scree. Fortunately most of our mountains are neither all one thing nor another, but offer a blend of challenge which you can turn to best advantage on the day.

You could test yourself on the south-south-east face of Beinn Bhuidhe, which is steep yet relatively safe. You won't ever need to climb anything steeper unless, of course, you want to, and if you find this comfortable you can then walk forth in confidence. For a variety of reasons, not least for the full view of the whole mountain afforded on the final approach, I prefer this route to either of those documented in M.

And as for estimating journey time, I use the very simple rule of 2 m.p.h. average over the horizontal distance. For example, if the map distance is 25km (approximately 15 miles) my first attempt estimate will be 7½ hours. This is crude, but has the advantage of involving only a single parameter, and can, therefore, be easily remembered and applied.

There are many factors which can now be added to or subtracted from this estimate to hone it into shape. If there is more mountain than walk-in (Bidean, for example) you may need to add up to 40% to the initial figure. If there is more walk-in than mountain (Carn an Fhidhleir coupled with An Sgarsoch, say) then you may do better than 2 m.p.h.

What you must do is establish a basic figure that fits your own style of walking, faster or slower as you prefer, and then embellish it with as much factor as you feel a need for, taking

On top of the world on top of Argyll – Sara and the author at Bidean's summit.

into account, as well as the above, weather conditions, physical geography and the possible need to find spring water on a hot, sunny day. With increasing experience you will develop the ability to make very accurate predictions of journey time in most cases.

It is also helpful if you can use the map to visualize the terrain, and here the comparison of one map with another can offer a great deal of insight, particularly as you grow in competence. Cultivated areas are clear. Look also for signs of bog, scree, boulder fields, barren plateaux and deep cut ravines. Every least kink in a contour line will tell you something. Then compare your mental picture with what you find on the ground, and learn from the experience.

But this is not a precise science. Even without injury, back-tracking, getting lost or any other potential hazard there will still be times when, inexplicably, your carefully prepared estimate will be grossly wrong – in either direction. It's all part of the joy and mystery!

On this matter, it is interesting to consider the accuracy of M's times. M gives 2½ hours for Driesh (we took 1h 35m straight up the 'front'), 3½ to Mayar (2h 35m, agreeing exactly on the traverse) and we were back at the car in 4h 10m (no M time for this). Our prediction, based on 8 horizontal map miles at 2 m.p.h., had been 4 hours. Not a bad result.

Over longer distances I find I go out faster than M, often reaching the first Munro in, say, under 2 hours against his figure of 2½, but slow down during the day so that over 8 to 10 hours I have pulled back level. If you start with M as a benchmark then you can adapt it as required to your own understanding of your own likely performance over the distance.

You will have realized by now with all this talk of miles that I am an unreconstructed imperialist. One learned feet and inches as a first language; metric came later. As such, I still prefer to think in imperial units – indeed, the Munros are thus delineated – and translate into metric if and when I need to.

On the assumption that you are of sufficient vintage to share this link with the past – that you are one to whom a 2,250' col speaks more clearly than one at 700m – then I offer the following simple method of converting metres to feet in your head. Since no one else has, to my knowledge, put this into print, I hope you won't mind my referring to it as Pete's Rule.

The Rule is:

To convert metres to feet, multiply by 3 and add 10% or add 10% and then multiply by 3 – it doesn't matter which way round you do the sums so you can let the awkwardness of the numbers dictate this.

Example: our 700m col linking Druim Dreirie with Bheinn Bhogaidh:

700 x 3 = 2100. 10% of this is 210. The imperial equivalent, therefore, is 2,310'.

The mathematically precise answer is 2,297', showing an over-estimation of 13' by the Rule.

Further example: the saddle at 820m above the head-wall of Coire Cnapain:

Add 10% (82) to get 900m (approx.). 3 x 900 = 2,700'.

The mathematically precise answer here is 2,690', an error of 10'.

Final example, and a real mountain at last: the height of Ben Nevis at 1,344m:

3 x 1344 = 4032. 10% of this is 403. The imperial equivalent, therefore, is 4,435'.

The actual height, as you will remember from school Geography, is 4,406'.

The calculation the other way about:

10% of 1344 = 134. Add this, getting 1478. Times 3 = 4,434', the slight difference being due to dropping the decimal place from the 10%.

You will see that the answer is always on the high side, but is accurate to within 1% of the precisely calculated result. This is true anywhere in the world! If you are faced with awkward numbers then round them down before doing the arithmetic. Take a top of 636m as 630, for example – you won't be far out.

In proposing such rules I am assuming that you are comfortable with this sort of mental arithmetic. It seems to me that the education system has done nothing for the younger generation in denying them the skills to do this type of thing in their heads. It was very pleasantly drilled into us as youngsters, without pain or punishment, and the dullest in the class could rapidly add up such a string of numbers and was proud to be able to do so.

Hazel was in a shop recently which was offering a 10% discount on several items. The electronic till, which would have computed this automatically, had broken down. Neither the assistant nor her manager had a clue where to start in calculating, never mind applying, the reduction. The customers were doing it for themselves. How does this generation know if it's being short-changed?

Even now I can add up a column of figures in my head more quickly than my children can do it on a calculator, and with a much greater probability of getting it right. This is not exceptional ability – anybody who has been properly trained can do it. We seem to have denied young people access to this form of mental acuity, but maybe it's not important.

While treating the matter of approximation it is worth pointing out that, with the magnetic variation now less than 5° east of grid north, and swinging down to zero and then up to 5° west of north sometime in the second half of the next century, it is not unreasonable to take magnetic north as equalling grid north.

Of course, if you need greater navigational accuracy – and sometimes you will – then you will know what to do anyway. If you don't, you are now spared the chore of remembering, for the rest of your lifetime, whether to add or subtract the wretched thing!

Do note, however, that this approximation is not necessarily valid outside the UK. Not everybody's grid north points in the same direction!

The wild card in all this planning is, inevitably, the weather. Your views on the forecasters' abilities will have been well formed and I shall keep mine to myself! I do keep a barograph running at home and have done for several years. I can now forecast changes in the Edinburgh weather about three hours ahead, this by a combination of what the chart shows, a dash of local knowledge and an old wives' tale or two. Extrapolating this to the mountains is far from straightforward, particularly when they can have their own mini-climates, but I have found a correlation between local weather and that in the Highlands east of Rannoch Moor. Also a high is a high and may, possibly, be relied on even in the West!

It is worth spending a little time discussing coming down – a matter usually sidelined by most authors.

The descent is as worthwhile an experience as any to be had

in the hills, and there is no reason not to savour it fully. You have achieved your plan. You have overcome pain and potential danger. You have triumphed over adversity. At fifty-something you have just proved to yourself and anyone else listening that you can still do it!! You are exhilarated. You have pushed yourself 'to boldly go' – to quote the world's most famous split infinitive – not quite where no other man has trod before, but maybe your particular choice of route is, in some respects, unique.

You are also tired, both mentally and physically, and in no position to be hurrying on. Your planning must allow sufficient time for the return, and as much thought and care should be devoted to it as to the ascent.

Consider the following:

Quality of Experience

You may not have had time to pause and view on the way up. You may have felt that time was running out, the climb more difficult than you imagined, and have succumbed to the imperative to press on. Now you can slow down. It is late in the afternoon with that quality of light which softens everything in its amber glow. There are views to be remembered, future climbs across the strath to be surveyed, the jumble and juxtaposition of nearby peaks to be reconciled with the map, distant lochs to be identified. You have invested much in coming this far. Your time is precious and limited. You will want to wring every last drop of value from the experience.

Physical Aspects

If you come down too fast you may 'cream cracker' your knees, as a friend of Sara puts it. You will need your knees for your next excursion – they will serve you better if not thus creamed. Our limbs are antique and need to be carefully cosseted. The rocks in that boulder field which this morning you skipped gaily over, from point to point with balletic poise, now seem much larger. Strange how the boot has to be lifted higher now to avoid tripping over them. It's heavier too. That upper strand of wire in the deer fence – during the day someone has raised it by at least 4″. Also, those stepping stones across the burn – some must have been swept away since this morning's crossing!

Even if you use the route of ascent it now seems very different. Do I remember that bend in the path? Where's that huge monolith which we identified as a landmark? Remember that when looking downhill you may not be seeing the whole slope, particularly in bad light. Look for tell-tale changes in the colour of the vegetation as indicators of discontinuity. Refer to the map and, once again, read between the contour lines. If you can have a good look at your route of descent on the way up then so much the better. Modify your plan as necessary in the light of what the actual terrain is doing.

Have you got enough water? Feeling dehydrated? Now could be the time to search out that pure mountain spring to recharge the flasks – you are still high enough for it not to have been polluted.

Here is another Pete's Rule, to be used, as ever, judiciously and where appropriate:

> The time of descent is 70% of the time of ascent to an equivalent level.

Example: It took 3½ hours to reach the summit of Sgurr a' Mhaochaid. You have spent the last 2 hours traversing its sinuous and complex main ridge and are now poised to descend from its West Top, Stob h-Ear.

Time of descent = 70% of 3½ hours, i.e. 2½ hours in round figures.

I have found this rule to be particular helpful as M rarely, if ever, gives the time to return, nor the overall journey span. Do please remember to adapt it to your own circumstances, and make due allowance for differences in terrain and for any final walk back to the car. As with all these 'rules' try them out, gain experience, and then modify them with your own findings as appropriate. Treat them as starting points where no better information may be available.

It is, of course, necessary to have a reliable, but not your best, dress watch. I carry a quartz one which cost only a few pounds but keeps perfect time. It is kept permanently on BST as it would require a PhD or the expertise to set a video player to adjust it, neither of which I possess. The remembering of this adds extra spice to winter climbs! Its plastic strap has long since disintegrated under the onslaught of winter cold and its face is cracked into various star patterns after being much dropped and retrieved. After one such episode the liquid crystal display disappeared altogether – there was just that bland, blank face staring back at me as if sulking after the violent abuse. However, it has real personality, carries on regardless, and I will not be parted from it. It even survived a machine wash, having evaded Hazel's pocket search after a particularly muddy outing.

Mental Aspects

You are euphoric but tired. A trip or slip now could sprain your ankle, or worse. Concentrate hard – banish any notions of switching into auto-pilot. Your judgement is suspect. If difficult decisions have to be made then sit down, sheltered if necessary and possible, take off your rucksack and pause and reflect.

Consider every aspect of the decision. Don't panic. Do you think you are lost? Where were you when you were last certain of your position? How did you get from there to here? Compass bearing? (Check it.) What can you glean from the lie of the land, the flow and confluence of burns, and any cliffs and visible peaks? Would it be better to return to that point and start again or to soldier on from here?

Bear in mind that in drought conditions lochans will have sunk and shrunk and might not have the same shape as shown on the map. A single expanse of water may have been reduced to a summer string of pearls. Are there higher tide marks to aid reconciliation? Remember that in fog things are never quite what they seem at first sight. Looming features look loomier; down may look like up. Apply the usual approach: gather as much quality information as you can, plan, analyse risk, review, decide and then act.

Nowadays, of course, you need never be lost. The GPS is with us and offers 100m accuracy provided you press the right buttons and the batteries aren't flat! I am too old a dog to learn these new tricks, and the technology seems to take all the fun out of navigation. However, it is obviously the way forward – in all senses – and must be taken seriously.

Debriefing

As soon as possible after returning home review the day's activities. Do this with the map. Why did you, perhaps, miscalculate the steepness and complexity of that glacial wall? That rocky outcrop you had to work round – what does it look like on the map? Could you have predicted its existence? What about from the 1:25,000? Why did the ascent take longer than planned? Should I modify my crude method of calculation or were there specific circumstances which will not recur? With hindsight, would I have planned it differently? In summary, what can I apply to future planning to make my expeditions safer, more predictable and more enjoyable?

And finally, the maps may need some minor repair work around the edges and folds – do this as soon as possible and they will give you good long service.

If you use M as a planning aid – and I strongly recommend this – you should recall that I have used the word conservative about it, and I use it to mean safe. If you aspire to being more adventurous you will take this into account in your preparations. Here is an example.

The final sentence in its description of climbing Creise and Meall a' Bhuiridh reads, 'Return by the same way.' This, of course, means reascending the two Munros so I was moved to consider alternatives. The ascent of the latter had gone according to plan – 1½ hours to the summit from the White Corries car park – helped by the starting altitude of over 1,000'. I had left Edinburgh early and was well into the climb by 8 a.m. It was one of those days where the beauty is breathtaking – clear, sunny and warm – the Buachaille looking at its most impressive in summer verdure. The barograph had shown a high over Scotland which was obviously in no mood to rush away, and as the day began to warm around Tyndrum my senses began to tingle at the thought of the pleasures ahead. The whole route was clear – just a matter now of deciding how to come down. I even considered leaving maps (for two are required for this one), compass and most of the kit in the car and doing it unladen.

Just as well not. Within reach of the top a chill thick mist blew in from Rannoch Moor and I needed the compass to determine the way off. Here an interesting coincidence came to light. One fold further west on OS 41 but in almost exactly the same relative position is another hill called Meall a' Bhuiridh, albeit smaller than the Munro. This was the one which came first to my attention on opening the map and I was totally confused by the rearranged topography until the lower spot height revealed what had happened. Fortunately it was not one of those gale- and sleet-driven moments when one exposes the map for the minimum possible time. Had it been I may well have made false deductions from wrong assumptions. Be careful!

ONE EXPOSES THE MAP FOR THE MINIMUM POSSIBLE TIME

The fog became intermittent and finally lifted completely, clearing the way for a survey of possible descents from a variety of angles. There seemed to be three options. First, the climb down the north-east spur of Stob a' Ghlais Choire. This started steep and got steeper. It looked more than a match for my capabilities. Secondly, the descent down the easier bit, followed by a south-easterly drop into the east-facing corrie. This would mean navigating some serious-looking scree. Thirdly, the climb

down into the same corrie from the saddle between Stob a'
Ghlais Choire and Creise. I chose the latter. The first 300' or
so are very steep, the sort of gradient which it's much easier to
climb up than down, but there were firm footholds in the dry
grass and many solid rocks for support. The return to the car
park was completed over the flat platform of Creag Dhubh –
from which there is a splendid view of Ben Nevis showing what
I call its Odeon Cinema profile – followed by nearly a mile of
gentle descent over the steep north-facing lower slope of Meall
a' Bhuiridh itself.

There were just three things to watch. The descent east into
the corrie needs to be continued long enough so that when
turning north one is below the steepest part of the east face of
Stob a' Ghlais Choire. Secondly, it may be unwise to get too
close to the Allt Cam Ghlinne, which is deeply ravined in that
section, and thirdly, there are three or four loose scree gullies
to cross which require due care and attention. If you aim to
cross the Allt at the northern end of the ravine, you won't go
far wrong. The crossing point was a place of great beauty and
stillness and the water tasted just wonderful. It might also be
possible to descend further east to the top of the ravine onto
its own mini Tonto Platform (for those of you who know the
Grand Canyon) and simply follow downstream, but that you'll
have to find out for yourselves!

Now this was all done in midsummer. Even so, there were
still some small snowfields lying in the corrie. In the winter I
would no doubt take M's conservative advice. Know what you
are capable of, make your own judgements and be adventurous
within the considered limits of risk analysis. There is not much
adventure in simply following other people's routes, and M's
are now becoming downtrodden and, in some places, heavily
eroded. You could, of course, take the chair-lift. No one has
yet given me a definitive answer as to whether this is considered
acceptable in an aspiring munroist. I would regard going up as

cheating. Coming down I haven't done either but know that others do. You must set your own standards – after all, it's being done purely for your own satisfaction and interest.

My plan for the day had been to take in Meall Ghaordaidh on the way home, subject to weather and general fitness. The latter was about to be put to the test. The Black Mount round trip, including the side excursion to Clach Leathad, had taken exactly six hours. Thus I was back at the car by 2 p.m. Meall Ghaordaidh was hardly a day's work and I had originally considered coupling it with Tarmachan. I had no particular desire to join the convoy of caravans and coaches trundling across Rannoch Moor which I had seen but not heard from up aloft. Most of it, no doubt, would be descending Glen Ogle, and dear Callander would be jam-packed with summer Saturday visitors, causing the usual half-mile or more tail-back into the Pass of Leny. The Munro would take about four hours which, allowing due time to drive there, should put me beyond all traffic hold-ups on the return trip to Edinburgh. Go for it!

I did. It was tough. Very few Munros are pushovers. No doubt the morning exertions had taken their toll, and one is climbing almost fully 3,000′ from the Glen Lochay side. The convex hill showed several false summits. I finished it by leaving the ruck-sack by a prominent rock and taking a reverse compass bearing on what appeared at the time to be the summit. Finding it again was an interesting experience, even with the bearing. On the way down all prominent rocks looked very similar!

The total round trip was 3½ hours. It had proved to be a most interesting, challenging, fulfilling, tiring and far from con-servative day. There was a singular reward, however, as I caught sight of my first and only red squirrel in Scotland in the pines on the lower slopes. Callander was traversed at 8 p.m., still going like a fair.

CHAPTER IV

Times and Seasons

One major omission from the discussion on excursion planning was the influence of time of year and, in particular, the differences between summer and winter climbing.

When Andrew and I climb together we set our dates well in advance. We find it necessary to book the time in this way, otherwise diaries soon fill up with conflicting arrangements and it becomes difficult to find time in common. Thus climbing days are much looked forward to and, although we take note of the weather forecasts and what the barograph is doing, we invariably go. Who knows, the weather out there, possibly 100 or more miles away, may be better, and we are not always disappointed. Rare are the days when nothing is achievable, and the gaining of an inconsequential Top in the most arduous conditions, braving everything that the skies may throw at us, has its own distinctive satisfaction.

We apply this approach in winter as well, the major difference being that the initial planning will have taken into account a reduced objective. In the early days we made few concessions to conditions as such, and allowed only for the shorter daylight hours. With increasing experience however, it became clear that the great summer collections were not, in general, going to be possible and that one Munro plus one Top would be an average and very worthwhile winter achievement.

Our best winter score was 'The Glen Lyon Four', including all Tops, during one fine January day. We started at first light and just made it back to the car by nightfall – a seven-hour round trip. On the way we abandoned an option to tack on Schiehallion as well! (I did say 'Plan bravely'!)

Those of you who think that crampons are private things used periodically by ladies are probably best advised to abandon all thoughts of winter climbing, go out in late spring, summer and autumn only, and skip to the start of the next chapter. Or you could choose a southerly approach in March or April, picking your way around any danger, and avoid the accumulated drifts of the northern exposure. That way you can savour the winter experience with little more risk than in summer, but watch out for cornices when you hit the ridge!

Those who have no knowledge or experience of how to use an ice axe to control a slide are similarly advised, for the time will come – be in no doubt about this – when you will need to know and put it into practice.

Snow, of course, in all its shapes and forms, is a major factor in any winter excursion. The existence of cornices and the potential for avalanches is well understood and presents additional challenge and risk to be evaluated, even in fine weather. The icing of the tundra on an otherwise easy gradient now makes it demanding. The icing of a steep pull makes it no longer a hill walk but a technical climb. Falls become more likely, and you will fall further, faster and could become buried. All these factors add to the assessment of risk.

You will have to decide when and where to use your crampons, and whether to keep putting them on and taking them off as you move from hard ice to bare rock. Removing them will give better balance but must be accompanied by the removal of soggy mitts, grappling with the fittings and the near impossible task of reinstalling the mitts over intractable fingers, all, of course, in high winds and sand-blasting sleet. And then, of course, the whole thing in reverse when you reach the next ice field!

What may not otherwise be appreciated is that a snow or ice field unpunctuated by rock or vegetation and with no visible footprints or paths across it has no discernible shape. Even with a horizon it is not immediately obvious whether the field is convex or concave, or even, from one's vantage point on terra more firma, whether it starts up or down. A degree of circumspect prodding is therefore desirable before committing one's boot to it.

This effect is heightened in fog, where disorientation can be total. There is no horizon, nor any other point of reference apart from the compass. This is a quite incredible experience, and well worth having – once. If these conditions seem likely to persist, I now have just one guiding rule – down, as fast as is safely possible, by the safest possible route, on the compass.

It is also important to realize that even quite large expanses of water can disappear from view totally when ice-bound and snow-covered. In such conditions the use of lochans as a navigational aid may not be possible.

On the credit side I must recall the exceptional quality of winter climbing on a good day, the quite splendid range of scenery above and below the snowline, the exhilaration that you will know from simple sledging with the children in your local park but magnified a thousandfold, the absence of midges and other winged nuisances, and the fact that certain terrain – the squelchy, boot-hungry bogs of summer – is now frozen solid and can be traversed with much greater certainty and speed.

On the matter of estimating journey time, I use my summer parameter of 2 m.p.h. to compute the length in hours and then add between 40% and 100% to get a winter figure. It is not possible to say beforehand where within that range to pitch it – it will depend upon conditions prevailing at the time. Therefore I simply use double summer time to provide an initial estimate of when I expect to return and have found this to be entirely satisfactory. I also plan my return to base to give me at least one hour of daylight in reserve. Although the eyes adapt well to failing light, the winter twilight is surprisingly short if you take the summer's as standard, and you will undoubtedly share my desire never to be caught out after dark.

Within this general framework one is usually back ahead of schedule, while enough slack is built in to allow for the sort of sudden and unexpected emergency, or just simple plodding slowness, that a winter excursion is apt to produce. It is worth specific mention that hard-won progress through deep snow in winter corries – up to your oxters in it – is greatly energy-sapping and soon leads to fatigue. This itself is a danger, for there may be no quick way to an easier route.

One of our most memorable winter or, more precisely, early spring climbs was on an occasion when Jo was staying for the weekend and expressed an interest in doing some hill-walking. She was fresh from ten days tramping the Dolomites and Andrew considered her good for a shot at Ben More and Stob Binnein. I thought that she would be more than just good and would probably outpace us. We had had the pair in our sights for some time and couldn't think of a better way of introducing a fit young lady to the delights of the Scottish Highlands.

We took a northbound line, straight up the nose of Stob Invercarnaig. Before the start, however, Jo discovered one of the simple rules of setting out from Edinburgh – a nature call must be attended to before anything else. She was obviously not used to this – the Italians must do it differently. We found her a large and convenient rock, assured her that there would be no further cars on the dead-end road at that early hour of the morning and duly mounted guard. Needless to say, she was just getting into her stride, so to speak, when one approached. The Law of Sheer Cussedness, well known to all O grade chemists, clearly applies in the hills as well! (See Apocrypha 4 – 8 for further details on this).

That was a magnificent day out. For the first time in our lives we experienced being sunburnt behind the ears, as the pull-down hats we were wearing had bent them forwards and exposed hitherto virgin territory to the blistering ultra-violet. Towards the end Jo was clearly tiring fast after the two Munros and Tops, and Andrew volunteered to go on ahead and move the car. This saved her a mile or so's walk back along the road after about eight hours hard work in the sun. On the drive back to Edinburgh we had planned a detour to show her the Forth bridges. When the time came she was fast asleep on the back seat, however, and we decided not to disturb her.

By the fourth winter of our quest we finally decided that we would heed the forecast, believe the barograph and henceforth confine our excursions to those days where there was the best chance of some fine weather. We had had our fill of trying to emulate Scott of the Antarctic!

We didn't need to keep proving that we could navigate our way all over Scotland in thick fog; that maps get shredded in high winds; that bad weather, winter outings with no worthwhile views had become an unpleasant chore; that cars left out for hours in wild weather don't like to start and, when they do, take ages to heat up and that, in such conditions, windscreens are reluctant to clear; that changing into dry clothing in the car is bad for one's head and back, and that changing into dry clothing outside the car makes dry clothing wet and thus negates the reason for changing in the first place; that driving in wet clothing is not a life-enhancing experience; that foraging for bridge money in a wet pocket presents unique challenges which are not worth repeating; and that it will take the best part of next week to get everything sufficiently dry for another outing to be possible.

Also, we had completed our research project into the high altitude performance of chocolate bars at low temperatures – their dramatically changed taste, their unusual crystalline structure, their relative hardness compared with our teeth, the intransigence of their wrappers – and had no further need to collect experimental data.

But by now, of course, we were over 200. Almost into the home straight. Downhill all the way from here, or so it seemed. We would now make up for all those days of horror. All subsequent climbs would be undertaken in the best possible conditions. The final push would be nothing but sheer enjoyment, with physical and other rewards to match. That's why we climb mountains, isn't it? I'll tell you later!

CHAPTER V

Equipment

By now it will be realised that I am a day-at-a-time excursioneer. I am prepared to concatenate, say, five days but these are subject to the general principles of manhood. Those of you undertaking seven-day hikes down the coast of Wester Ross and camping each night will have different needs, and I can safely assume that you are old enough and ugly enough not to need my advice anyway!

If you carry into the mountains all those things which the literature tells you are required, you'll never get airborne! That comment is not intended to imply irresponsibility; your own planning and risk analysis, based on increasing experience and competence, will be your guide. Leaving aside clothing and footwear, which should need no comment from me at all, given the stated scope of this book, but to which I will return later to discuss one specific aspect, I will take four items invariably. These are map(s), compass, drink and food.

Everything else I regard as optional. You must make your own subjective assessment here, deciding on a cost/risk ratio acceptable to yourself. If you are prone to ankle strain or suffer greatly from snow-reflected glare your conclusions may be different from mine. If, like me, you have a mild back problem (and who doesn't at our age?) you may prefer to travel without assuming the configuration of a camel.

I have done somewhat more than half my Munros without carrying a rucksack. This admission has surprised many people but I can assure you that it has worked well for me. I am much more likely to wear one in the summer when potable water can be difficult to find from natural sources, and a few extra pints of liquid may be required to avoid dehydration on the longer excursions in hot weather.

For winter climbing I carry two further items, an ice axe and crampons. The latter can be suspended from the waist band if not worn, the former held tomahawk style if not used. Thus the rucksack may be totally dispensed with in winter, for which course I advance the following arguments:

❊ If I am accompanied by Andrew, who likes to carry one, he can be my Sherpa.

❊ In any event a winter's day will be planned as no more than six hours and, therefore, one will never be more than three planned hours away from the starting point.

❊ Dehydration is rarely a problem in these circumstances.

❊ A full backup kit of dry clothes, food, drink and medication will be available at base.

❊ It is easier to return in conditions of difficulty unencumbered.

❊ I am quite prepared to turn back with objectives not accomplished if, in the conditions of the moment, I judge it foolhardy or unacceptably hazardous to continue. There is no loss of face in doing such, and the mountain will always be there for another attempt.

For the record I have done this on two occasions only. The first was on Beinn Dubhchraig with Sarah and Lisa. They desperately wanted to climb a Munro. I had chosen that one to give them a relatively easy ride to the 2,000′ mark and to see what they were capable of. If that part of the ascent proved successful we could then tackle the steeper final section with confidence. Also, their Melbourne suburb contains Black Rock

Point, the coincidence of name making this mountain particularly appropriate. The weather was atrocious and worsening but the ladies fought hard to succeed – I would expect no less of Australians. However, it was not to be. The upper mountain was sufficiently snow-bound effectively to deter them and I had no need to exert my right of command. They looked a splendid pair of drowned rats!

The second time was in similar conditions with Andrew on Meall Glas in unrelenting fog. We had reached the top of something but it was not cairned or marked in any other way. Leaving Andrew as my beacon I had systematically explored in all directions – the land fell around us on every side but the slope and distances were difficult to assess accurately in the conditions. This was the nearest we have come to being lost and was a salutary learning experience. Down on the compass was the only realistic option and it was a relief, after what seemed to be an interminable up and down descent, to emerge from the cloud at a recognizable point and with a welcome view of Auchessan Farm. We met a somewhat bedraggled party by a sheep fank, bent on making the ascent. Our unequivocal advice was gratefully accepted – conditions by then being considerably worse.

I returned as soon as possible afterwards in good weather to retrace the route as exactly as possible using our original compass bearings. Several knolls could have qualified as our 'top' and I was relieved to find that we had not strayed too far from plan and, had we continued, would duly have reached the ridge to the summit. However, I have never regretted the decision to turn back.

Curiously, that mountain coupled with Sgiath Chuil is much more difficult than a study of the maps would have one believe. I'm not sure exactly why this should be so, but maybe the longish boggy approach is somehow more demanding.

The revisitation also taught me a useful lesson about over-confidence. From the southern prow of Sgiath Chuil there was a clear sight of the route down, right to where I had parked the car, for the road was under repair at the time with one-way traffic controlled by lights. The matchbox vehicles first being queued and then allowed to pass had been a constant feature of the views back to base. There was no need for navigation, therefore, and the map and compass were stowed away and the descent undertaken on auto-pilot, with the brain engaged on other important matters such as putting the world to rights.

Suddenly things were not right at all. The view had gone and I was on the wrong side of the wrong glen, and it was becoming very precipitous very quickly with the steep walls funnelling me ever closer to the torrent. To retrace would be the easy recovery, with a chest-high crossing above a waterfall and quick traverse one strath westwards. How different it could have been in Glen Coe ... Wee Jimmy working the lights back at the car couldn't quite believe what he was seeing as this human bog rat stumbled towards him.

We finally mastered Beinn Dubhchraig one Boxing Day in superb, sparkling, winter weather. It was one of those cold, sunny days where everything in the mountains is highlighted – the snow on the old Caledonian pines, the icicles overhanging the waterfalls, the views of other mountains in their winter covering, the exhilaration, the family banter – a day when it feels especially good to be alive. The party included Andrew, Sara, Rupert, Nick and Greg. The American lads looked some- what incongruous, as our supply of winter gear had to be supplemented by a motley array of alien and ill-fitting outer garb, but all were kept very warm.

Andrew had the ice axe and led, cutting steps as required. This enthralled the cousins, who had never experienced anything like it before, despite their early Canadian upbringing. They described the whole experience as 'cool' which was at the time, I'm told, the highest accolade an American youth will confer on any experience, and comes with special merit if that experience is being provided by someone from across the generation gap.

I did suggest that 'cool' was quite an appropriate way to describe our ice-bound ascent but, on the whole, Americans are too literal-minded to warm to that sort of pun.

The plan had been to include Ben Oss as well but, as often happens on these occasions, modern youth is happy to settle for less than is possible. They had great fun coming down, using their outer garments as improvised sledges and, with Strath Fillan well in view and there being not much in the way of danger which hadn't already been pointed out to them, I quite happily relinquished the tight control of my party which I would normally have demanded.

And now, to return briefly to my earlier comment on dress.

One of the great virtues of hill-walking is that it can be practised by all comers. It does not require a huge investment in clothing and equipment, other than that which is already well enough known. I would hate to see our sport hijacked by commercial interests as has happened, say, to cycling or skiing, where the participants are made to feel inadequate unless they flaunt the latest in designer label turnout.

I started simply with old trousers and thick jumpers, but always took care to ensure that the underwear was thermal and comprehensive and had all the necessary facilities. (A somewhat feminist friend of Hazel – an enthusiastic walker of the Pentlands – asserts that the only time she has any sense of penis envy is when she needs to pee in the mountains!) Even now, I use little in the way of specialist clothing, everything being usable by any member of the family at ground level except, perhaps, for a pair of screed-out breeks which nobody would want to be seen alive in!

I can buy boots in Edinburgh at a fifth of the cost of a product with identical functionality but with the name of a well-known athlete blazoned on the uppers. Now, I have nothing against this athlete. I just prefer the other four-fifths of the price to remain in my bank account and not be transferred to his or his agent's.

I am greatly amused by those who consider that 'my clothes, my watch, my car, my home' – and so on for as long a list as you would want to put together – make a statement about 'me'. None of us is really that important in geological terms. I wear clothes in the mountains to keep warm, dry, safe and to be fleet of foot. I am making no statement! If you wish to spend more than you need to on these things then that is your privilege entirely, but if you don't then you should certainly not be denied your full and rightful enjoyment of the mountain experience. Anyone who suggests otherwise either has no understanding of the quality of this experience or is simply trying to profit from your ignorance!

CHAPTER VI

Access

Here I want to address the matter of how we get from home to the start of our climb.

Home, of course, is Edinburgh. If you live in other parts of the country you will need to make your own adaptations to what follows. I well remember a discussion with a local climber on Conival to whom even the Grey Corries and Glen Coe were remote.

By road from Edinburgh there are three main arteries to the climbing fields – the M8 west to the Arrochar Alps, the M90/A9 north to the Monadh Liath, Cairngorms and the north-west of the Great Glen (with side trips into Perthshire for the White Mounth and east of Rannoch Moor) and the M9 for the rest. Options are often available. Whether you approach Ben Nevis, for example, from Glen Coe or Glen Spean is partly a matter of personal taste and partly a matter of how you want to climb Ben Nevis. However, I do try to keep out of Glen Coe during the tourist season.

The M8 is the least useful for an Edinburgher. There is a point somewhere in Glen Falloch which is the mathematical mid point to which the mileages from Edinburgh via Stirling, Callander, Lochearnhead and Crianlarich and via the M8, Dumbarton and Tarbet are the same. Anything north of, say, Beinn Bhuidhe is probably best approached by the former route unless you are particularly addicted to motorway driving.

The A9 north of Perth is difficult when busy. The arguments

How you want to climb Ben Nevis – Andrew on its dark side with Carn Mor Dearg (the Red Mountain) behind.

for and against dualling it all the way to Inverness seem evenly balanced and I have no strong views about this. I am quite happy to leave it to the politicians, who demand that we pay them ever more handsomely to make difficult decisions on our behalf. I have found myself on occasions, for example, returning down Glen Tilt late in a summer's evening and hearing the constant hum and whine of traffic on the Blair Atholl bypass, wondering if the residents were not, in fact, better off before the new road was built. On the other hand, there are plenty of places where dualling would have a limited environmental impact

What I do feel strongly about is that if people drove the road with proper care and consideration then it would be much less of a nightmare, without a great deal of money needing to be spent on upgrading it. However, hom. sap. motorens seems genetically incapable of altruistic behaviour, to which the pedestrian in any city will be able to attest. If this is true of h.s.m. generally, then h.s.m. (var. towbarii) is, as they say, something else.

Here is a typical A9 scenario during the tourist season. A motorist towing a caravan followed by a food delivery lorry bound for a well-kent supermarket outlet in Inverness, followed by ten other assorted vehicles, enters the first dual carriageway stretch north of Perth. The lorry and ten assorted vehicles pull out into the outside lane to overtake h.s.m. (var. t.), but the road is now going downhill and h.s.m. (var. t.) discovers a second wind. The battle is now on, and we watch it enthralled from our grandstand place at the back of the queue.

At first the lorry seems to be gaining, but no, h.s.m. (var. t.) is holding him, creeping ahead, even. Now the lorry is pulling ahead again, then falters. The tension is mounting. Who will overcome? It's neck and neck – must be decided on a photo-finish!

A motorist towing a caravan followed by a food delivery lorry bound for Inverness, followed by twenty other assorted vehicles, now enters the next single carriageway section, the latter twenty ready to take their chances along it to the next piece of dualling, or perhaps one should say, duelling.

If you venture forth onto the A9 for any distance you will usually be able to rejoice in such an experience, and this can be true at any time of the year. If you venture forth very early in the morning – as you will often need to do if you are doing a day trip to remote parts – then ice on the road is a potential hazard in the winter and spring months. I have often been the first thing up the road on such a morning and found it like a skid pan. Do take care.

There is a splendid piece of legislation in California which requires any driver with five or more vehicles behind him to pull over at the first possible opportunity to let them pass. This, in practice, works well and, since California is a society palpably more selfish than our own, I see no reason why it shouldn't work well here also. We do this on the single track Highland roads as a matter of course, using passing places to allow overtaking, but the lateral thinking required to apply it to the A9 also just does not seem to be part of h.s.m's. (of any variety) corporate ethos.

For those of you interested in a closer study of this aspect of human behaviour the A9 is rich in examples of the following types, and they can, when observed, give as much pleasure as the spotting of a large herd of deer in some remote glen.

The Sedentary Scene Spotter

Unlike ourselves, prefers to do his sightseeing from within the vehicle, which he drives at no more than 40 m.p.h. His positioning on the road is usually such that he can be overtaken on the inside in total safety.

The Marginal Muncher

Likes to picnic at the roadside, as the particular quality of the air there imparts its own special flavour to his food. Usually identified with nearside wheels on the verge and offside remaining on the carriageway, thus making overtaking a non-trivial event.

The Bedtime Blazer

Wants to get home quickly at the end of the day and tends to regard travel at less than 90 m.p.h. as a grotesque infringement of his personal liberty. He usually drives so close that you are unaware of the full-beam headlights until after you have pulled back into the nearside lane.

The Bashful Braker

This variety doesn't like his stop lights to be seen at all, so he occludes them with a rack full of bicycles with thick tyres. These are usually slightly wider than the vehicle itself which, again, makes overtaking a worthwhile challenge.

The Informal Enforcer

Most frequented habitat is in the Dunkeld area. Likes to insert himself from a side turning at the head of a queue of traffic quite happily moving at the 60 m.p.h. legal limit in the mistaken belief that by slowing it down to 40 he is making a significant contribution to road safety. Take care not to confuse this one

with the s.s.s. if you join the queue after he has applied himself
to the head of it.

The Old or Young Pretender

Likes to drive a vehicle environmentally adapted to the Australian outback, believing that this will deliver the real wilderness
experience without his having to make any hard physical effort.
Quite harmless, but can be difficult to see round. In high
summer he may assume the plumage of the bashful braker.

One other thought I have about the A9 is that if Hugh and
Sheila had lived in, say, Strath Nethy rather than Glen Lonan,
then Pitlochry would undoubtedly have become our Callander,
and I do hope that, in saying that, I am not offending any who
belong to either place.

Pitlochry is a fine town, well worth a stopover, and it would
not be reasonable to compare one place with the other feature
by feature. There is one interesting parallel, however, in that I
tend to regard Ben Vrackie as having the same relationship to
Pitlochry as Ben Ledi has to Callander. It, too, is a splendid
mountain and, although not a Munro, well worth a few hours
of anybody's time.

While on the matter of road access to the mountains I should
just like to say a few words about hitch-hiking. This may be
thought of as a high-risk occupation, both for the hiker and the
hikee, but I have used it to good advantage on several occasions.

The first was on a splendid day when I had finished the three
Munros and three Tops of the Newtonmore end of the Monadh
Liath by lunchtime, had no particular wish to come down as I
was enjoying myself so much, and Geal Charn was seven miles
over there to the south-west, unplanned, but requiring not much
in the way of loss of height, so why not?

That all worked brilliantly but left me high in the Spey Valley, some ten miles from the car. The return walk was engaged but, just after Laggan, I was mercifully rescued by a couple of rock-climbing Edinburgh University students who were now Inverness bound. One preferred to return to Edinburgh anyway and so I traded my lift for his – a good symbiotic relationship.

On another occasion I was very kindly taken most of the way along the private track from Dalwhinnie to Ben Alder by another Edinburgh graduate – this one a geologist collecting data in the area – and at least half the way back by a local family from Kingussie. It certainly turned that walk in and out from a chore into a pleasure, and I am grateful to them all   anonymous friends in need that rekindle one's faith in humanity.

Glens Shiel and Cluanie are places where, if you are to take full advantage of the possibilities, you may end up miles from your starting point, and I have hitched up and down that road several times, usually being picked up by fellow climbers recognizing the need. As a drenched, soggy thing one hardly appeals to the driver of the pristine Merc as an occupant of his recently vacuumed passenger seat, and who can blame him for passing by on the other side?

Likewise, I do my bit for the cause, picking up people who appear to be bona fide walkers needing this form of support or, indeed, anyone who looks half reasonable, so far with no ill effects. But if you do hitch-hike I recommend that you face the traffic and engage each potential lift with eye contact. A denial then has to be a personal refusal rather than the passing of a turned back. I wouldn't expect hitching mams to be perceived as a threat by oncoming drivers – idiots, perhaps, but not dangerous – so you should succeed where others might not!

One thing I do feel strongly about road travel is that, after a hard and tiring day's work alone in the hills, one may not be in the best physical or mental condition afterwards for the drive home. Rather than increase the danger to myself and fellow road users (even h.s.m.t.!) I have considered and used the railway system on a number of occasions. Here are some possibilities for you to think about.

From Blair Atholl station walk (or hitch – this was one of my non-successes, being passed by two cars showing no interest) up Glen Tilt to climb Carn a' Chlamain and Beinn Dearg, to be back at the station in time for the afternoon train. This is a bit of a slog, with the most interesting part scenically being the initial walk-in.

On these trips I divide my load into that to be carried and that to be left at the start, the latter including food, drink and a change of clothes. I found a disused coal shed near the station to conceal this, placing the rucksack clear of foraging animals (or anybody else).

I have also used the West Highland Line to approach the Arrochar Alps from Ardlui or Tarbet stations and, in so doing, discovered a wonderful ScotRail anomaly. That is, the cost of a day return from Edinburgh to, say, Ardlui is 70% more than the sum of a day return from Edinburgh to Glasgow and a day return from Glasgow to Ardlui. There are questions to be asked, therefore, before arriving at the best deal!

At that time the early train from Waverley rejoiced in the title of 'Lord of the Isles' and went straight through via Glasgow. Unfortunately, the vehicle itself never quite lived up to this magnificent title, being just a standard, prosaic, diesel-driven bus-on-rails staffed by a conventionally attired crew. But, at that ungodly hour, it didn't seem to matter.

One of the main problems with this approach is that the return trains are timed to leave at around 2.30 and 6.30 p.m., with nothing in between. The former is too early to get the best out of a winter's day and the latter involves hanging round the station for two hours of darkness – but at least the heater in the waiting room was working. How about a train at 4.30 p.m., ScotRail?

Travelling by train to the mountains usually occasions at least one amusing incident. After a thoroughly wet and horrible twelve conclusive rounds with Beinn Narnain I needed to persuade the Inspector that the soggy yellow and red rectangle with indecipherable writing on it which I produced from my breast pocket was, in fact, the return half ticket. The man on the train from Tarbet, who knew what Beinn Narnain was, believed me; the man on the Edinburgh train, who didn't, didn't!

THE MAN ON THE
EDINBURGH TRAIN ... DIDN'T

One most memorable railway journey involved an early departure by car from Edinburgh to connect with the 8.36 a.m. Glasgow-bound from Fort William at Tulloch station.

The grand plan was to take the train to Corrour halt – virtually inacessible otherwise – and walk back over Beinn na Lap, Meall Garbh, Chno Dearg, Stob Coire Sgriodain's South Top and then the Munro itself, all of which looked a good day's work. I had arrived in Tulloch at 8 o'clock, well in time to down the usual flask of tea and get kitted up. That branch of the West Highland Line was to be a new experience and the usual excited anticipation of what the hills might have in store was enhanced by the obvious pleasure of the unusual approach.

Tulloch station is well in the Swiss-chalet tradition of Highland railway building, albeit a former shadow of its fully active self. Although the integrity of the architecture is well enough preserved with the buildings in reasonable condition, resident staff have become an unbearable overhead to the running of such a venture, and so the former booking hall and other station facilities are no longer functional. Information comes from a telephone linked to the control centre at Banavie whence came the good news that my train was on its way.

In a siding sat a railway vehicle the like of which I had never seen before but which was clearly and cleverly adapted to its Highland environment. The central portion was a yellow box on wheels with windows on all four sides. Pointing one way along the track – I can't really refer to its front or back – was a snowplough and in the other direction a backhoe.

Nor was the station deserted. In the now defunct ticket hall or, possibly, waiting room were a dozen or so railway gangers occupied over tea, cards and morning papers, obviously ready to start their day's activities once my train had passed through. I spoke to their leader, distinguished as much by his *Guardian* as his clear authority, when he emerged to make for the yellow box. 'Yes, the train had been on schedule throughout the week and should be in very soon now.' His confidence added to the comfort offered by the telephone.

I took up position at the up, both in geographical and railway terminology, end of the platform facing down the straight line ending with its gentle left-hander curving away down towards Spean Bridge. Stob Ban, shining in the sunrise, benevolently stood watch. The autumn sun had already warmed the morning air and the peaceful, tranquil atmosphere was suffused with a delicious, almost indefinable, sense of expectation. Highland High Noon at 8.36 in the morning – and you could almost hear the Tiomkin music!

The appointed time duly came ... and went. A second reference to Banavie elicited that the train was in some difficulty at Spean Bridge and a suggestion to call back in ten minutes or so when a diagnosis, if not prognosis and cure, might be available.

A great deal of telephoning was now going on among the gangers and soon enough the head man emerged to elaborate the news that I fully expected but fervently prayed might be otherwise: 'Train's broken down at Spean – door's fucked.'

Now I must pause here to explain that word in some detail, if only to reassure those of you who normally wouldn't utter such language. It is not used here as an expletive but economically conveys whole layers of meaning. These may be summarized approximately as follows.

Firstly, the door is broken in such a way that it is beyond the powers of those on the train to mend it. Had he said 'Door's buggered' this would imply that repair, to the extent of a workable solution, could be engineered locally and the delay, therefore, would be relatively short. The problem here is that the train itself is disabled until the automatic door has indicated itself to be safely closed.

Secondly, it means that those capable of dealing with the matter are not immediately to hand and will need to be detached from their present activities, duly assembled in one place and then transported to Spean Bridge station with all necessary tools and equipment.

Thirdly, this will all take a relatively long time and the train will most likely be delayed hours rather than minutes.

Thus the word is used in contexts where deep meaning must be conveyed succinctly while the speaker is under pressure. Another good example of this is the use of the term 'away' in polite Edinburgh society. 'Fred's tummy's away' said of a friend's husband in explanation of why they couldn't make it to lunch actually means 'The poor bugger's had his bum on the bog all night, his head in the basin barffing, and didn't know which end of him to deal with first!'

Our leader had now boarded the yellow box and fired it up, a smoky, spluttering, coughing, diesel-inhaling, Highland megabeast which he skilfully piloted out of the siding shuddering and shaking and onto the main line, bringing it to rest at the station platform. In piled the crew.

'Are you going to Corrour?' said I to one of them.

'Aye, and beyond.'

'Could I please come with you as far as Corrour?'

'I'll ask himself,' and 'Aye, jump in.'

I was duly helped inside, probably the most dangerous climbing manoeuvre of the whole day, and it was this piece of inspired good fortune opportunistically seized, together with the kindness of the workers themselves that duly delivered me to my intended destination only fifteen or so minutes later than the regular service would have achieved.

In this context and company I now rate the train journey up the east side of Loch Treig as one of the great railway experiences of the world. The views from the yellow box were truly spectacular and came with the added advantage of the all-round panorama. To the gang it was nothing, however, and, after hearing with incredulity and due examination of the maps my plan for the day, they continued their waiting room activities of cards and morning papers.

Also of interest to me was the head man's involvement with the radio token system which allowed us to proceed in safety up the single track to Corrour without fear of being endangered by another railway vehicle coming down the hill towards Tulloch. Long gone are the days of relay baton passing on the West Highland Line.

After dropping me the yellow box continued on, belching and wobbling like a drunken dinosaur towards Rannoch, and I heard it return to disappear again back towards Tulloch as I was crossing the 1,750′ contour. On reaching the 2,500′ cloud base I lost the view back to Corrour halt. The 8.36 from Tulloch to Glasgow Queen Street was still nowhere to be seen.

And after Stob Coire Sgriodain, how to get back to the car at Tulloch station? The road from Fersit is devious and that sort of walking is never particularly attractive anyway. Cross-country the track shown on the map soon disappears into impenetrable thicket and, anyway, river crossings have to be considered. I did the obvious, but please don't tell my friends in the yellow box!

You can also consider using this railway to Fort William and beyond – I did 'The Glenfinnan Three' this way – for the journey itself is spectacular and, although the train takes longer, it surely wins over having to drive in summer holiday traffic. And if driving is inevitable you can always use for your return the by-ways that were the A9 before that artery was upgraded. They parallel the newer road in several places and offer a much more tranquil trundle than its frenetic pace will allow.

One other aspect of access to the hills which should be borne in mind is that we are always moving over private land – for even mountains are owned by somebody – and whether this is individual or corporate ownership doesn't make a great deal of difference. I have heard others' horror stories about confrontations with landowners but can relate no such experience. In all cases where I have needed to consult local opinion I have been treated with the utmost courtesy, and offered every reasonable facility, even in the open seasons. Maybe I've been lucky, or maybe it's a matter of approach. There should be room in the hills for all interests to be served without conflict, and I see little reason why this should not continue to be so under the current traditional access arrangements.

An amusing contradiction was the 'HILL CLOSED' injunction at the foot of Ben Hope, as if it were a cafeteria facility which would reopen sometime tomorrow, perhaps around lunch time! How much of Sutherland did its author wish to 'close'?

Finally, a quick word on bikes. I have never used them but, clearly, certain long and less than spectacularly interesting approaches can be substantially shortened by using pedal power. I harbour a certain puritanical view that they are a mild form of cheating, but will leave you to your own decision on this matter. What I do hope, however, is never to see in the Highlands the brutal churning up of paths that we find in the Pentlands. This may now be just a pious hope. Have you seen Glen Affric recently? I am thinking of that section lying beyond the 'NO WHEELS' notice.

CHAPTER VII

Californian Interlude

It is always interesting to compare the Scottish climbing experience with that available in other parts of the world and, as a fairly frequent visitor to the western US, I had long harboured hopes of doing some walking there when a suitable opportunity presented itself. The Sierra Nevada range separates California's own Garden of Eden in the Sacramento and San Joaquin river valleys from the wild desert country to the east – Death Valley, and the state of Nevada.

The range itself quickly declares its glacial origins, with gentler slopes to the west riven by natural wonders such as Yosemite National Park, and a steep escarpment facing east. This side offers the easiest access to Mount Whitney, the highest peak in the Sierra and, at just under 15,000', the highest in the US excluding Alaska.

Unfortunately none of our friends or contacts there knew much about how to go about it and so the whole thing began to assume the proportions of a trip into the complete unknown, and it was, therefore, planned from first principles.

Although it is possible to acquire the necessary maps in the UK, these have to be ordered, so I decided to buy them once in the US rather than end up here with the wrong thing. All one could effectively do, therefore, would be to pack boots and the usual clothing and equipment, and do the real homework on the other side of the Atlantic.

Although no one in the map shop had attempted Whitney, a

great deal of good advice was offered, the key piece being to register one's interest with the local forest ranger's office, local here being the town of Lone Pine on the north/south road lying east of the Sierra which links Los Angeles with the playgrounds of Lake Tahoe. One of the first differences one then discovers between Scotland and the US is that a wilderness access permit is required to camp overnight in the National Park.

In fact, we were originally told that one was required just to enter the Park but this proved to be false. As with any such set of enquiries it is wise to ask questions this way and that of a variety of more or less competent opinion until some sort of consensus emerges. We had almost moved mountains to arrive at the office before the appointed deadline, only to find that it had closed an hour earlier. Dark mutterings about government cuts to the US Department of Agriculture's Forest Service were heard – not so different from back home, really.

The closed office was not a problem for the form-filling, as the necessary documents were available outside the building – even to the extent of a courtesy ball-point pen – and a copy of one's details, including intended route, is posted back inside. However, the opportunity to discuss the tentative plan and listen to some up-to-date advice on current conditions was denied, for the start on the mountain was to be at 6 a.m. the following morning.

Even though I now knew that the permit was not necessary for my own limited excursion, nevertheless it seemed a good idea to fill one in as it would leave formal documentation of where I was expecting to be in the event of my non-return. I was later disabused of my naive assumption that the whole permit system was designed to ensure the safety of the wilderness wanderer and account for his safe return, by various Republican-leaning friends muttering their own dark thoughts about government employees' make-work, looking for ways to justify the continuation if not expansion of their empires. Again, not so different from home.

It was May and daylight lasted from about 5 in the morning to 8 p.m., but with little in the way of twilight at that latitude.

The road towards the hills from Lone Pine ends after eleven miles at a forest car park with extensive camping facilities for those who want to go up the night before. However, as a mam and his wife, we had luxuriated in a motel back down in the valley, and were setting off dry and well rested. The car park was at 8,300′ leaving around 6,700′ of ascent – just a couple of Munros, one on top of the other! – over a distance of some twenty-two miles. Not impossible, you would have thought.

I failed for several reasons.

Firstly, the mountain was more snow-covered than not, much of it quite deep. I had not brought any winter gear and had to search for safe ways round several steep snow and ice fields which would have been straightforward with ice axe and crampons.

Secondly, I had ignored the ranger's advice posted to a tree on the lower slopes to ascend the upper mountain by way of a steep gully to the col from which the summit would be reached, as it appeared to need the winter equipment which I had left back in Scotland. There is a well-made path from the car park to the summit but it was mostly under snow. I had tried to use this instead of the recommended gully, but the face up which it zigzagged was too steep in the prevailing conditions and the path was only infrequently discernible. During the summer the rangers put safety ropes at the more dangerous reaches.

Thirdly, I was not sufficiently adapted to the altitude. This only became clear in retrospect, and is not a problem which ever bothers us in Scotland.

Fourthly, I didn't have enough liquid. I was following my usual winter practice of climbing without a rucksack, and had carried a flask for the first 2,000′ of ascent. The plan was to fill this with stream water or snow melt. The former was ruled out by local opinion as likely to be contaminated, and the latter refused to melt and made a disgusting looking brown porridge around the iodine pill which local wisdom had also recommended.

Finally, I was going to run out of daylight unless I turned back soon. Navigating the route and looking for alternative ways around snowfields had taken their toll, and it was as well to be prudent. One of the other differences between Scottish and American climbing is that if you need to be rescued you will have to pay the full cost of this yourself, and it was not going to be covered by my insurance.

I didn't even make the col and had turned back at around 13,200', just under 300' short. I returned without the benefit of the view over the other side of the mountain. Although disappointed, I try to be philosophical on these occasions. Much had been learned, and Whitney would remain for another day. I had accepted before the start that my planning had been totally inadequate and would need to be conditioned by the experience itself. The initial outing I was prepared to treat as a recce. I would find out what needed to be done to achieve the objective on some return visit. If the first had taken me to the summit, that would have been a tremendous bonus.

The successful attempt came exactly one year later – same season, same general weather conditions – clear blue sky turning to azure as one gained height, cold never a problem and just a light wind – perfect, in fact.

This time we had stayed in the area for a few days to acclimatize. I was now fully equipped with rucksack, liquid and winter gear. The plan included intermediate targets, realistically set after the previous year's experiences, against which progress could be monitored and the likelihood of success or failure constantly assessed.

On reaching the Whitney Portal car park we were reminded of the wonderful smell of pine which hangs in the area, much more intense that anything in Scotland, even among the native stands. In fact, with the well-made and marked path available to any walker, there are some splendid and rewarding views and wildlife experiences accessible to any climber's companion who prefers not to spend his vigil back in Lone Pine or elsewhere.

I had set off half an hour earlier and was at the foot of the gully at 10.30 a.m., five hours into the climb, and by now well clear of the scented pine forests of the lower mountain. A party of four American men passed me on the way down, having set off even earlier and made a successful ascent. They told me that the record for Whitney had been set a few years back by a young marine – 4½ hours. The mind just reeled at the thought. In most fields of human physical endeavour the determined amateur can come to within a decent percentage of the achievement of the professional, or even the world record, but this was breathtaking. I cannot conceive that I would ever, no matter how hard I might train, come close to even twice that, but this will probably never be put to the test.

My friends also told me that I hadn't a cat-in-hell's chance of making it to the summit. By now the waist-deep snow in the steep gully was mushy under the strong morning sun. Like them, I would have needed to be up at the col before the daily melt had started, taking advantage of the hard surface to do that part of the climb as quickly as possible.

'Fuck you,' I thought, through a beaming smile. 'No mere American is going to tell me what I can and can't do!' Nothing like such a provocative challenge for an additional motivator. They did give me one piece of useful advice, however. Crampons would not be needed for the rest of the journey. I thus discarded these and various spent liquid containers, hiding them to be collected on my return.

What the Americans had missed was that I could use their steps up the gully: they were sufficiently compacted to provide firm footholds. One hour later I gained the col.

It was a breathtaking moment, both physically and metaphorically. I was higher than last year. I saw the view behind the mountain for the first time. The path down into the wilderness is named after our own John Muir, who was instrumental in persuading the US Government to set up the national parks system. My path continued along the ridge, only intermittently visible under the snow. I was glad that I had kept the ice axe. It was never needed as such, but provided great comfort over the next half-mile or so, which was dauntingly steep on both sides. The route is, however, technically straightforward.

The col is at 13,480′ and lies about a mile and a half south of the summit. A mere 1,500′ to climb, but this is where the effect of altitude began to make itself felt, particularly after the rigours of the gully. This was very much into the unknown for me, as I had never operated at such a height before and had never put my limitations to such a test. Subsequently I read Rebecca Stephens's account of her final approach to the top of Everest and now know exactly what she meant.

After the first wave of pain I established a routine. Do twenty paces and rest on the ice axe. Don't look up – it won't be any nearer. Deep breathing. Twenty more paces – try thirty – it won't work, stupid – stay in control. Rest. Don't look up. Deep breathing. Twenty more paces. Repeat.

At one of the rests I was aware of somebody standing watching me. 'Say, fella, how ya doin'?' It was the ranger on the way down.

'I'm exhausted, I don't think I can do it.'

'Sure can – just keep goin' – ya'll be there in twenny minutes. Just be sure ya get back acrarss the ridge before the surn goes over the hurrizon an' the snow freezes urp again.'

This was exactly the encouragement I needed. I also had Hazel's final words to consider: 'It's now or never. I'm not coming back to this place again just to wait while you make yet another attempt.' (With all due apologies to Lone Piners who, no doubt, consider their place to be the centre of gravity of the universe!)

Up and over the final summit dome was an experience to savour, and then, of course, there were the views. Those to the west had been with me for the two hours or so of the final trudge and were a constant inspiration. The vastness of the place is difficult to convey. It has something of the quality of Torridon, but with real forests, and huge at that. Nothing man made in that direction, just a mosaic of sandstone ramparts, tranquil lakes, finely sculpted glens and the trees themselves, all highlighted in the snow. The scene was constantly changing, partly as a consequence of my slow, staggered progress and partly as the sun beat its own more measured path through the heavens. The whole was capped by the deep indigo sky canopy, something we don't ever see in Scotland at our relatively lower heights.

To the east, far down the mountain, Lone Pine was just discernible. Then there were the ridges beyond – the Inyo Mountains and the Panamint Range. But for Telescope Peak, the highest in the latter, it might have been possible to see down to the lowest point in the US, just under 300′ below sea level, in Death Valley.

In the earlier stages of the ascent I had regularly passed and been passed by a pair of teenagers who seemed to have greater commitment than most I saw on the nursery slopes to finishing the job. They were singularly ill-equipped for the purpose, even to the extent of wearing shorts. At the foot of the gully I had thought it prudent to offer some well-constructed and well-meant advice and guidance.

'Fuck you,' they would have thought, through beaming smiles. 'No mere Brit is going to tell us what we can and can't do!'

They had decided at that point that one would wait there for the other to return – not a bad piece of altruistic behaviour on the part of the former – and from the col onwards I had become

the informal and unofficial guardian of the latter. If he was
going to get severely burnt legs, about which I could do nothing,
at least I could protect him from the other dangers. It was
helpful to me also to have something else to worry about apart
from my own pain. I had decided, though, that if he fell I would
not go down after him and put us both at risk in my weakened
state, but go for the nearest climber with a portable phone,
failing which, the first camp on the way down, and call help
from that point. I was comforted by the notion that my brain
was still sufficiently in gear to be able to deliver the clear thinking
needed to devise such a strategy.

My young friend was ahead of me to the summit and we
exulted together in that sublime feeling of having overcome all
resistance. We had climbed the highest mountain in his country
and would probably live to tell the story. He would linger on,
savouring the experience, while I started back, knowing that the
regaining of the col was now my major objective. He was faster
than me and would soon catch up. Meanwhile, I would shepherd
him from in front.

There is a well-constructed shelter at the summit which comes
with a warning notice to stay clear during thunderstorms. You
can climb Mount Whitney during August, virtually snow-free
and using the path to avoid all difficulties. However, the main
danger is from the weather, which is very changeable at that
time of year. The warning notice was applied to the shelter after
someone was struck by lightning while using it, and successfully
sued the Government (or his heirs did) for compensation. That's
how they do things in America!

Digressing somewhat, I have a plan to walk down to the
bottom of the Grand Canyon and back up in the same day.
This is definitely not recommended by the Ranger Service who
would prefer you to spread the venture over two days, and I
think it has a lot to do with an official fear of being taken to
the cleaners by those involved in mishaps. America is way ahead

of us here, but we appear to be catching up quickly and, I must admit, I find myself totally lacking in sympathy for those who would wish 'the Government' to take responsibility for all their life's vicissitudes.

I had prepared well and knew exactly the route, the timing and the pacing, as well as what victuals to take. I reviewed my plan with the rangers and threw in the fact that I was fresh from, if not flush with, my recent Whitney success. They reluctantly and cautiously agreed that it could work but, 'Be sure ya make it back urp – I doan wanna havda come down an' haul ya out.' That plan is now in abeyance, awaiting a future visit. It's like doing Nevis upside down – first the descent of 4,500', then the reascent. The main problem will be the heat, sun and possible dehydration. Route finding is easy; the Americans run mule trains up and down for the wealthier tourists.

Back down the gully on Mount Whitney my young companions were reunited, but not me with my crampons or water bottles. An extensive search yielded nothing and I had neither the time nor the energy for anything further. Whoever took them I hope is finding them useful.

There are two formal campsites on the lower mountain, one at just over 10,000' and the other at 12,000', just below the gully. It is above this point that one senses being in the real wilderness, there being nothing else of human construction apart from the path between here and the summit. Both camps sport a pair of chemical toilets, well hidden, and well camouflaged with sandstone coloured paint. These facilities seem to work efficiently and solve a problem which, here in Scotland, we prefer not to think too much about.

The young pair raced ahead to their parents' car and, as I came down the last few bends of the final zigzag on the tourist path, I heard the most almighty bollocking being administered by the father. It was just dark. I decided not to intervene – guardian angels have their place and this was not it. The lad would be elated with his success and could look forward to telling his grandchildren all about it when the time came. We waved each other goodbye.

The round trip had taken 14½ hours – just ten hours outside the world record! What a day!

We applied one final lesson learnt from the previous year and spent that night in the welcoming motel rather than making a dash for our next planned Californian destination. That day's experience needed to be caressed carefully and savoured at length.

Hazel had an illustrative tale to tell of her entertainment during the day. She had sought out the City Park in Lone Pine – you soon get used to the idea that everything in the States larger than Dalwhinnie is referred to as a city (pronounced siddy) – to which she repaired with her book and modest picnic, having decided that she had otherwise exhausted possibilities of the place during our previous visit.

Across the green there came a' huffin' and a' puffin' this grotesque, overweight, pot-bellied, sweating man followed by his equally obese wife, of such a size and disposition that she exhibited the greatest difficulty in keeping up with him, and several assorted and unkempt offspring, all bawlin' and brawlin' – a sad portrait of the Great American Dream Gone Wrong. They were desparate to secure the last remaining picnic table – which they did – and spread their burden as widely as possible over it, to allow not the slightest possibility that any other person could remotely conceive that he might share this space while they toiled back to the car for the next load. Now we had the blaring radios, the portable TV and an assortment of mangy, mauling, grumbling family hounds.

Full ownership of the table having been secured, they spread out their meal and began devouring it, rich in carbohydrate and accompanied by disgusting looking, rainbow coloured fizzy drinks, with several beers out of the bottle for himself, all punctuated by a rich assortment of zoo sounds and other varied ejaculations.

As if cued by destiny, the park's automatic high pressure sprinkler system suddenly cut in, aimed directly at this rabble, who and whose food and electronic noise were comprehensively and forcefully drenched. Back to the car they staggered, never appreciating the poetry of the justice, nor the amused European view of their antics.

About two months after this Whitney excursion Sara was in Africa and had attempted Mount Kenya. She made it to about 15,000′ but became too ill to reach the summit. She was only some 2,000′ short.

My own experience at these heights is severely limited and I know very little about who may be more prone to altitude sickness, whether it affects certain folk rather than others, and to what extent such characteristics are genetically determined. By her own account she seems to have been much more severely affected than I was, even though she was well enough acclimatized to the height. More research is clearly necessary. Mount Kenya – here we come!

And one final thought on Whitney. During the morning I had passed many young hopefuls, all bent on making the summit. They were splendidly arrayed in their designer clothes, dark glasses, headgear, gloves and boots, and replete with shiny new crampons and flashing ice axes. Some were so devoid of technique that they were destined simply for a pleasant romp in the snow on the nursery slopes; others were moving at a pace which didn't give them a chance. We exchanged the usual pleasantries together with transatlantic greetings as I passed by ('You from Scartland – say, is that part of England?'!) and left them way down the corrie. Nobody who came behind me on that day reached the top of Mount Whitney. I was the last.

CHAPTER VIII

The Cairngorm Test

It seems that Knights of old, as well as Kings and Princes, were sufficiently solicitous for their daughters' virginity to keep them hidden away in the high turrets of their ancestral castles. A Lorimer lock-up, as it were, to deter the most ardent suitor. Serious contenders for the hapless hand were then set daunting tasks of derring-do in which, if successful, they would be allowed to plight their troth in earnest seriousness. I have always raised a smile at the use of the word 'plight' in that context.

Perhaps the scaling of the vertical walls would suffice – it would certainly be appropriate for a mam – or the winning of battle honours, or even the retrieval of a lady's slipper.

Such thoughts came to mind as I was leading Dieter up Ben Macdui.

Sara had invited him to stay for the weekend and had announced that, as she was working all day Saturday, he would have to amuse himself until she came home. I had planned to be in the Cairngorms anyway and he jumped at the chance to come along.

We have so much in the way of climbing clobber at home that we can usually kit out a visitor, even to the extent of finding a pair of boots that fit. It was mid-September so there was no need to go so far as to provide all the winter gear. He did end up looking like something dressed by a theatrical costumier, however, but nevertheless declared himself to be comfortable.

KEEP THEM HIDDEN AWAY IN THE HIGH TURRETS

Dieter is a fit young man, a Zimbabwean well used to the rugged outdoors of Africa, and not in the least bit troubled at the thought of spending most of a Saturday doing strenuous things in the company of a potential father-in-law.

However, experience teaches one not to make assumptions about the mountain capabilities of untried guests and, in order not to put them into difficult positions yet still gain something for everyone from the day's work, I usually look for an easy and gentle start with no rough edges, as it were. Thus my original plan was modified along these lines. When I had seen what he was capable of I could then include more or less as seemed appropriate.

We set off for Lurcher's Crag with the intention of walking the high ground to Ben Macdui via its North Top. In Dieter's presence my mountaincraft would need to be exemplary, so we did all the required map and compass work by the book. On my own I would have taken it as read. He was most impressed with all this as it was something new to him. I was glad that we had done it properly, for the North Top and the Ben itself soon disappeared under a cold, clammy, autumnal mist which then continued to deny us any view down into the Lairig Ghru.

We went out on the compass as far as Sron Riach and I had planned to include Carn a' Mhaim as well. However, this would take us yet two miles or more further from the car at Coire Cas with very little chance of seeing anything, so I decided to invoke a fall-back plan and return via the ridge to Cairn Gorm itself.

On the way the fog began to clear but we were never totally free of it. Thus there were fleeting glimpses down into Coire an t-Sneachda to our left and tantalizing images of Beinn Mheadhoin across the glacial trench of Loch Avon, away to the south-east.

Just before the summit of Cairn Gorm is the Edinburgh University weather station, continuously recording wind speed and direction and, at half-hourly intervals, automatically popping up from within its own cairned enclosure the instruments needed for measuring temperature and barometric pressure. It is a splendid piece of remote, unattended data collection, with readings sent automatically back to the University for computer logging, analysis and prediction. This is of inestimable benefit to mams, skiers and other mountain interests, and Cairn Gorm is one of the few places in the Scottish hills where you can get a fully accurate account of what the weather is doing at more or less exactly the time of asking.

The whole thing does, however, have a rather comical air about it, reminding one of a Dalek or other such space fiction monster, particularly on seeing it for the first time and not knowing what is about to happen. On a later visit I had briefed my companion on what to expect. It was a splendid warm and sunny afternoon and we were quite happy to wait, as if for curtain-up at the theatre. But nothing popped up. Perhaps it was lying dormant on that occasion, or the technology had been upgraded.

It was only after the outing with Dieter that the notion of the Cairngorm Test began to take firm shape. Subsequently any boyfriend arriving at the house was considered fair game by the other children, being told that, unless he could survive eight hours under the most arduous conditions being grilled as to his prospects and lifestyle by father, then he had no chance. In their own jargon he would be chilled, binned or axed, depending on the severity required. Joking apart, though, it's not a bad test of character for a prospective postulant.

By this time Rupert was already married to Vicky but elected to do the test retrospectively. Now it had been globalized and did not necessarily need to be taken in the Cairngorms. We went up to the hills west of Drumochter, intending to circle the four Munros there, but only managed as far as Sgairneach Mhor. It was the last day of October and the weather was atrocious. Snow was lying down to the pass and there was fog on top, resulting in a total white-out. I did not wish to bring the news to Vicky that I had lost her husband somewhere on the road to Beinn Udlamain so we turned back after reaching the summit.

Rupert would have continued; he is a fit young Devonian with plenty of experience of the wild uplands of Dartmoor, but I felt that he had done enough to pass! He later described the ascent as being like a never-ending staircase.

We arrived back at the car with fingers so frozen that we could barely apply the key to the lock. Despite this experience Rupert is now a frequent visitor to the mountains and is beginning to amass quite a respectable number of Munros. Perhaps the family tradition will continue ...

My next climb with Dieter was Inyangani Mountain, whose summit ridge we walked on Boxing Day, 1996. Like the Cairngorms, it is made substantially of granite, but the going is very heavy through the thick African undergrowth and fractured rocks. Inyangani is a mountain so holy that one must never point to it. If rocks or flora are disturbed they have to be reinstated quickly lest spirits be released to plague the local communities and wreak vengeance upon the perpetrator. Not all the challenges associated with climbing are technical!

It is in the Cairngorms that I have done some of my longest walks. This is a huge arena, with long walk-ins from the north, east and south but relatively easy access from the car parks of Coire Cas and Coire na Ciste, the approach road to which from the A9 doesn't quite manage to avoid the banal brashness of Aviemore. Its inner sanctuary around Loch Avon, a private place, is almost too good to be true. It can only be fully savoured after many visits and different approaches. It needs to be experienced in all seasons from above and below. It is a holy of holies, the beauty of which is quite beyond words to express. Had Debussy visited there, he would have written a piece of piano music to describe its sights, sounds and smells.

It was after one of these epic Cairngorm outings that I had

brought home to me the total alienation of the wilderness trekker from the civilized world. My return from the Lairig Ghru had been through the Chalamain Gap, then a straight line east across all obstacles towards the tourist path which heads away from the ski lodge towards Lurcher's. It was late on a summer evening, one of those occasions when full advantage has been taken of the long day – I was drunk on exhilaration and extremely tired.

There was a party on at the lodge and a group of revellers, splendidly clad in their dinner jackets and long dresses, had come out for a stroll along the path to soak up some of the warm evening atmosphere and view the last rays of sunset over towards Aviemore. Suddenly they saw this thing moving slowly across the bog, staggering like a wounded animal, but with human shape and movement. What was it? Could this be a Cairngorm Yeti? But it was only me.

The initial tension had now dissipated; only the incredulity was left. Yet they looked as incongruous to me in that wild setting as I obviously did to them. I rose up to the path and they almost visibly backed away. No doubt I smelt as horrible as they were perfumed. We had no other point of contact; words were not possible; there was nothing to say. I shuffled back to the car; they continued in the night air.

CHAPTER IX

Nationality and Nationalism

As incomers from the South we had been quite surprised at the intensity of the nationalist debate, both sides of which seemed to us to be well founded on several misconceptions. We had no doubts as to the differences between Englishness and Scottishness, and the fact that these were now to be given a much higher profile in our lives was something with which we inevitably had to come to terms.

I am writing this very carefully as I have no wish to offend any of our friends, English or Scottish, or anybody else, and certainly don't wish to be misinterpreted into any false position. I want to produce a book about climbing the Munros, enlivened with a few scattered excursions into various other related areas which might interest you, and the politics of nationalism or, indeed, of anything else, is not one I am choosing.

My mother was a Stobo whose own mother originated on Tyneside. She did her nursing training at the Royal Infirmary and one of her aunts was a permanent Edinburgh resident at the time. I have no doubt that early memories of her talking about the City as the only place on earth worth considering seriously, and taking it as her home, influenced me in seizing the chance to come and live here when it was offered.

There were also some quite strange coincidences. I was a frequent shuttler from London to Glasgow in the days before British Airways formalized that term, and we were almost without exception diverted to Edinburgh. It was as if she were drawing me close, showing herself to me, saying 'Look here! Can you ever conceive of anything more beautiful?'

Although this is being written somewhat with tongue in cheek, I do know of others who have felt impelled to make some of life's momentous decisions under similar feelings of compulsion, as if destiny was, indeed, preordained. As we battle away with whatever the world throws at us, I find myself seriously wondering to what extent we can be said to be in control of our own lives. This is a rich vein of thought which you can readily explore under the exigencies of Munro climbing, and I shall return to the matter again.

One of my early banking acquantainces in Glasgow was keen to establish the extent of my Scottishness. One major difference between Scottish and English banking – and I am generalizing – is that the former still treats you as a human being with specific, individual, even idiosyncratic needs and not just a credit score on a sheet of paper. As to how long this may continue to be so, I have grave doubts.

'Thirty-seven and a half per cent Scottish,' I averred, having done the genetic computation.

'Hmm,' he considered carefully and, after long pause for thought to make sure that the words he would use conveyed exactly the right meaning – what more could you ask of a banker? – 'That's probably just enough!' Thus naturalized I can now claim a foot in both camps, and use it as appropriate.

All of which brings me to this point. What is a Scot? What do those who graffitize 'Scotland for the Scots' or 'English go home' mean by these words? No proponent of either side of the nationalist divide has yet given me a satisfactory answer, and it's important for our children that he does.

For example, in Scotland v. England rugby and football matches they all support Scotland, of course. More profoundly, Sara was born in Edinburgh – a real native – yet genetically she is only half as Scottish as me. She was educated here and, not unreasonably, considers herself a Scot.

She took her first degree from Oxford and decided to apply to Bath University to do a PGCE. 'Why Bath?' we enquired.

'I wanted to be nearer home!'

'Sara, we know you are a biologist and not a geographer, but do you actually know where Bath is?'

At the interview she was asked if she had any preferences for her practical teaching.

'We could send you to Swindon, Trowbridge, Shepton Mallet, Chippenham, Bristol, Warminster ...'

'Oh, I don't mind,' she had replied, 'It's all just ... England.'

If the 'English go home' brigade ever have their way, to which home should she go when the pogroms start?

Another source of mild amusement in our family is the biennial '70% of Morningside occupied by the English' typical headline in the *Scotsman* newspaper, which, no doubt, does good business by this constant stirring of the nationalist pot.

Where are they? We have lived there for over twenty years and know a vast cross section of its population, many as dear, close friends. I can think of only one family which could be thus categorized. What is the *Scotsman*'s data base? Is there some strange selection process at work which causes us to meet and associate with only the 30% bona fide Scots?

This is a double calumny. Not only do they not say what they mean by 'English' but they've got the numbers wrong as well.

There are forces at work which seek to profit from our differences. It is an interesting and worthwhile exercise to identify and confront them. We can be so much more effective when exploiting our own common strengths than when we succumb to the divide and rule merchants with their own hidden agendas.

As an aside I will now admit to having reached a point in life where I rarely read newspapers, even the so-called serious ones.

When they are writing about things I know and understand in depth, I find the treatment so riddled with errors and so facile that it is a total waste of anybody's time to become involved with it, particularly those seeking further and better information about something of which they know little. By induction, this must apply also to those topics about which I know and understand little but may wish to learn more. I treat newspapers as part of the entertainment industry and take them on that basis.

I feel sure that any one of you will be able to recall experiences in which you have been involved, a public event, possibly, or as witness to an accident, and find yourself wondering when you read the press coverage if they are actually reporting the same happening. The search for Absolute and Objective Truth – more of which later – remains as elusive as ever!

While on matters national I should like to say a few words about Gaelic. All our mountains apart from Broad Cairn, The Devil's Point, The Inaccessible Pinnacle, of course, The Top of Eagle's Rock, Lord Berkeley's Seat, The Saddle and the newly invented Knight's Peak have Gaelic or Scots names, and I have at least made an attempt to learn how to pronounce them properly. This seems the right thing to do. Sheila gives instruction from time to time, and I can now say Buachaille Etive Mor – of which there is a splendid view from her lounge, looking over twenty miles straight up the great parabolic glacial strath bounded by the two Etive herdsmen – so that only a Gael knows what I am talking about!

The language is rich in words meaning hill and mountain – here are the ones used for the 3,000′ peaks: Aonach, Beinn and Bheinn, Bidean and Bidein, Binnean and Binnein, Braigh, Bruach, Bynack, Cadha, Carn and Chairn, Ceann, Cnap, Cnoc, Corrag, Creag, Cruach, Druim, Leathad, Lurg, Mam, Maol and Maoile, Meall and Mheall, Monadh, Mullach, Sail, Sgairneach, Sgor and Sgurr, Spidean, Sron, Stac, Stob, Stuc and Stuchd, Tom and Toman, with a few more to add to those to

cover some of the lesser hills. What a splendid range this is –
far more than plain English can muster – each one telling us
about subtle differences between mountains, and giving clues
as to their shape, size and general disposition. There is a smaller
list of Scots terms which could be added, and even this beats
the English equivalent. Indeed, many words from both sources
have been imported into English to make up for its comparative
paucity of invention in describing such features of the landscape.

Americans pronounce glacier as glaysha. There is no point in
talking to an American about a glassier – he won't understand.
So it is with Gaelic. However, life is never that simple.

I was heading up Glen Dessarry with the Chiochs and Sgurr
na Ciche in view or, rather, not in view. The farmer had very
kindly let me take the car beyond the point at which other
mortals are required to abandon their vehicles.

'Whither are you bound, my good young fellow?' quoth he
(or words to that effect).

'To Skoor na Keecha,' respondeth I in my best Sunday
morning Gaelic.

'Oh aye,' saith the farmer, 'Skurr na Quiche' (as in cold pastry
flan).

It is easy to feel sorry for the stalwart men from the North
of England, good mountaineers all, who rush up to climb
'Annick Begg' and then have to face the drive back down the
M6 to Manchester or Sheffield after their day's exertions. I
remember, particularly, Dave and Jack and their party of young
rock climbers from Oldham who shepherded me across the
Aonach Eagach. Their support and companionship were of
inestimable value and I am grateful for them. The next day they
were planning to challenge the north face of the 'Buckerlee',
for which I forgave them. I try and do missionary work on behalf
of the language but usually get responses of the form 'Eeh, if
Ah sed it laik that at t' clymin' cloob nowt'd oonderstand.' The

operators of the ski facility at Aonach Mor don't do the cause much good either.

My all-time favourite, however, occurred at the top of Ben Macdui during the administering of the original Cairngorm Test. A fellow cairn sharer with a very definite West of Scotland accent disclosed that he was now bound for Ben Medwin. Now, I knew the Cairngorms pretty well but had never heard of this particular peak. It must be some minor top which had not hitherto caught my attention. However, it seemed unwise to display any form of ignorance in the presence of Dieter, lest he lose confidence in my ability to lead him down out of the thick fog which engulfed us. I decided to find it on the map later, in fireside comfort, and so I did. You can work it out for yourselves, like I had to!

The original Gaelic and Scots name choosers were certainly fixed on the female breast. A' Chioch, Mam this, the Pap of that, Sgurr na Ciche all tell the same story, and the words trip gaily off the tongue. Would we in English, I wonder, name our hills Little and Large Bosom and manage to keep a straight face when speaking of them? It would surely raise a titter, if not a guffaw!

Mention of the Cairngorms also reminds me that The Devil's Point, just south of Cairn Toul, is actually a mistranslation – no doubt inspired by such inhibitions – of the Devil's penis. Whether you take such an anthropomorphic view of this Munro I must leave to your own judgement, but its shape did put one thing to rest in my own mind. As A level mathematicians we had to calculate the volume of the solid object formed by two intersecting cylinders. The calculation was straightforward; the visualization of what such a thing might look like was not. The Devil's Point provides some insight into this, its steep east ridge having thus been carved by the two intersecting glacial flows.

To the other side of Cairn Toul is, of course, The Angel's Peak, invisible from The Devil's Point. This must be as frustrating for the Devil as it is a relief for the Angel, and no doubt accounts for some of the rumblings which can be heard in the Lairig Ghru, from which all three are clear to see over a long stretch of that magnificent divide.

CHAPTER X

Antipodean Adventure

A ustralia's highest mountain is Mount Kosciusko, for which
I am using the local spelling and not the Polish one. At
7,316' or 2,228m it may be familiar to you as the world's
smallest tallest peak.

Australia has gone fully metric – all ms and ks and no ft and
mi – and I am, therefore, largely abandoning my imperial convention for this chapter only. When all about you are talking
and thinking metric it is both difficult and wilfully idiosyncratic
not to join in. If you are one who, when abroad, likes to convert
local currency in his mind to arrive at a meaningful understanding of value then you can use Pete's Rule – it works just
as well 'down under', and with the same less than 1% error on
the high side.

Later in the year that Andrew and I had climbed Ben Nevis
the hard way, he decided to join Philip – who had emigrated
in 1988 – and spend a year on a working holiday. Hazel and I
had planned to visit over the Christmas break – Christmas in
Australia, where the snow lies not at all at sea level, never mind
deep and crisp and even, proving a most fascinating experience
– and the notion of climbing our and their highest mountain
in the same year was conceived and took root. Philip would, of
course, join us to make a grand family outing.

Our forward planning was of a much higher standard than
for Mount Whitney as Ken W. very kindly provided maps and

information about the area, and we were able to investigate possible approaches well in advance.

Mount Kosciusko lies just to the north of a well-developed ski playground and is very easily approached from the south in exactly the same way as Cairn Gorm here is from the north. More easily, in fact, for a chairlift will take you from the Thredbo River valley floor at 1,400m to the start of a gently rising walk to Rawson's Pass, the Mount Kosciusko/Mount Etheridge saddle at 2,110m. Thus the mountain top is accessible to any reasonably fit person who cares to try it, and the ski resort offers, for an Australian dollar or two, certificates signed by the manager in validation and valediction of this achievement. You may rightly guess, therefore, that the path leading from the head of the lift to the mountain has become heavily eroded, and is now reminiscent of the tourist route up Ben Lomond.

The Australians have countered this by building a raised metal walkway over the distance of some four kilometres and placing other more sensitive areas where revegetation is being encouraged off-limits, all of which seems to have been very successful in allowing the worn areas to regenerate.

You may also rightly guess that this approach had little appeal to a mam and his sons!

Ken's maps showed a bulldozed track approaching from the east. This started at the end of the tarred road through Perisher Valley – another popular ski resort – which ends at Charlotte's Pass. The track was built to allow service vehicles access to Kosciusko from behind a locked gate, much as we are used to in the Highlands. However, we had hoped to find a route from the more or less virgin west, where there were no mapped paths and the terrain appeared rough and heavily afforested.

Some of my mother's family emigrated to Australia under the assisted passage schemes of the 1950s, and we have several Edinburgh friends who have made their home there more recently. Thus there is a substantial colony of friends and relations in the Melbourne area who give us additional incentive to make the journey, and whom I invited to join us on or to help us in the preparation of the Kosciusko trip, or simply organize the celebration party to greet our triumphant return. In the end we were a varied group of twelve, six of each sex, with ages ranging from the early fifties down to mid-teens. None of the indigenous members had any mountain experience, but Australian Tim had done some bushwalking.

The trip was planned to take three days, with the first and last doing little more than cover the outward and return journeys to and from Melbourne. We left at 6 a.m., broke for lunch and reached Dead Horse Gap, the 1,600m pass which separates the Murray and Snowy River catchments and lies just 7½km south of Kosciusko's summit, at 2 p.m. as planned. The Australians found it difficult to believe that we were already higher than anything in Scotland.

Andrew and I were to climb Kosciusko by this route to do a recce, assess the difficulties and then return east down the track where we would be met at Charlotte's Pass. Meanwhile, the rest of the party under Ros's command – she had made all the accommodation arrangements – would drive on into Perisher and set up camp.

The weather was dry but cloudy and the route clear except for the summit itself. There was a Cairngorm feel to the mountains with their mainly granite bedrock, but the vegetation – snow gums and alpine plants then unknown to us – told a different story. A clear path led us to the 2,000m contour from where the final pull to the 2,100m Ramshead plateau was straightforward. Climbing the granite tors presented the only real challenge.

Kosciusko would not, I think, claim to be one of the world's most exciting mountains. Distant views of it show only an undulating ridge with no clear point. Strzelecki is credited with the first climb in 1840 and gave it the name of the Polish patriot

– all of which is recorded on a plaque near the summit cairn. However, it is considered highly unlikely that Kosciusko had not previously been scaled by stockmen reaching higher and higher for yet more grazing land, and before that by the Aboriginal population during their summer migrations in search of the bogong moth for food.

Grazing of the high alp persisted into the middle of this century, and there are now major conservation projects in hand to repair the damage and restore the mountain landscape to a more natural state. If you do ever visit this part of the world, therefore, please take particular care to bring yourself up to date with all the various current regulations and recommendations covering access to and behaviour in the Kosciusko National Park.

Of much greater interest than the highest point in Australia would seem to be Mount Townsend and its connected peaks. Whereas the main Kosciusko ridge is, perhaps, the Australian equivalent of walking the White Mounth, the side trip to the north-west looks much more demanding and has some of the appearance of the high ground of Glen Coe.

This part of Australia is also of particular interest to the geologist, as it is only in the general area of Mount Kosciusko that indisputable evidence of the last glaciation exists.

One of the greatest challenges of this trip was to run it in such a way that everyone involved got something out of it. I had downgraded my original hopes of walking the whole 7,000′ plateau – with an approach from the uncharted west to make it more challenging – to the simple objective of getting twelve assorted individuals, with their own hopes and aspirations, to the top of their highest mountain and back down again in total safety. This outing was clearly not now going to be a rigorous mountaineering expedition on which personal safety would depend upon the coherence and commitment of the whole team.

However, some sort of team would need to be forged from this amalgam of disparate and unlikely material.

There were 'us and them' divisions visible along several fault lines – this and that generation, the Australians and the Brits, those in the white car and those in the blue, those of this and that family, those who were out to have fun and those taking a more serious approach, the men and the women – but we were all united by the general enthusiasm and hectic preparations of the week before in Melbourne.

As an aside, I have found it more acceptable in Melbourne to be Scottish rather than English if I need to specify the nature of my Britishness. If my Australian host is English he will welcome this; if Scottish, even more so. The unity is of a common bond standing firm together against the prevailing culture – something really quite subtle but, nevertheless, tangible. This all happens against an Australian background of debate as to the nature of Australianness itself and whether, as a specific example, that country would be better to go down a republican path rather than continue its current constitutional relationship with the UK. I do not expect this matter to be decided in the short term. It will probably occupy us well into the next century.

The equipment assembly and victualling were given careful attention, tents borrowed from cousins who would have liked to come but who were precommitted to other activities, meat for the barbecue apportioned and frozen, gallons of ale amassed and all set ready for our early departure. The team began to assemble from their own corners of the City and the excitement communicated itself to all members. I had decided on the following general management principles:

❖ The expedition should remain a pleasant memory for all participants for the rest of their lives.

❖ The answer 'yes' would be given to all specific requests whenever possible.

❉ The principal objective was that all would reach the top of Mount Kosciusko.

❉ Discipline would be light but firm.

❉ Decisions would be explained with reasons given for rejecting the alternatives.

❉ Special care would be taken when rejecting alternatives suggested by the less experienced members.

❉ Safety would in no circumstances be compromised.

❉ The whole trip would be fun for everyone.

❉ I would at all times be unequivocally in charge.

I could reasonably ask for the latter as it was generally recognized that I knew what I was doing, even in a foreign country, and nobody else in the party knew any more than I did. I took great comfort from the fact that Ros is a nurse, and that any illness or injury would promptly and properly be attended to. Like most I know in her profession she possesses that quiet competence upon which you know you will be able to rely under the most extreme conditions. She also has a great deal of practical common sense. She, therefore, became my partner and co-leader and between us, an Australian and a Brit, a man and a woman, we formed a very effective and unobjectionable command.

After the research excursion we had finally decided to walk the track from Charlotte's Pass to the summit – a distance of eight or nine kilometres – with a side trip to Mount Etheridge for the views and to make an otherwise quite prosaic journey more interesting. There were no technical difficulties of any sort; it was going to be easier to get lost or injured in a Melbourne suburb. At Kosciusko's summit the team would be offered a choice – either return by the route of ascent or complete the circuit along the north-west ridge to Mount Twynam from

Near the top of Australia – Philip R., Andrew, the author, Philip, Ros and crew on Mount Etheridge.

which Charlotte's Pass would be regained after a steeper descent. It was all very straightforward. We were duly met at the Pass and driven back to the camp.

Here a great deal of work had been done in our absence and the team had colonized an area close to a barbecue stand. My tent, christened 'headquarters' and shared with two of the younger men, was in the middle of all this.

It was now that skills which I didn't possess came to prominence, for which I was thankful and by which greatly impressed. There were those who knew exactly the right sort of eucalyptus bark to fuel the barbecue to impart the best flavour to the food, where to find it and how to use it on the fire. Others carefully tended the liquid refreshment, applying sufficient ice to keep it at its most drinkable temperature. Yet others had located the various bars available to the camp site and the shortest routes of access, both on foot and on wheels. The showers, toilets and drying facilities had been fully researched, and the evening meal was about to be prepared. The great range of talents of individual members, particularly those who understood the local way of the world, were now being harnessed to the common wealth, instinctively and without any particular process of management. Everybody pulled his weight or made her contribution.

There are many treasured memories of that evening and the one after, not least this fellowship and the feeling of unity in a common purpose. There was also a family of visiting possums who seemed quite happy to share our food and who added their own joy to the proceedings.

Above all there was the Australian night sky, full of surprises. We had now got used to the midday sun being in the north. You tend not to notice these things unless you have a need to know, as we do in the mountains. The first impression is that it's all back to front, the sun appearing to rise in the west and set in the east, until you finally remember why it is appearing this way.

But at night, in this location far distant from any source of artificial light, it was special. Here were those parts of the Milky Way never seen in Scotland, glowing with determined intensity. There was the Southern Cross away in the south, and constellations and galaxies I was too ignorant to name, and so were my Australian companions. And then there was the surprise of the burgeoning crescent moon looking like an open rather than a closed round bracket – obvious when you think about it, but a surprise none the less when you see it for the first time. Now we learned to separate Australian myth from Australian reality.

In one way I was quite glad not to have been involved with the matter of camp discipline. Tim had taken on this responsibility – he was a Military Policeman – and had, therefore, an authority which no Australian would have lightly challenged. Anything coming from me as a foreigner in this department and perceived by the natives as heavy-handed could have caused resentment, and had a discouraging effect on the morale of the team. There is nothing quite so fragile as human relationships and I was desparately keen not to have our great event marred by the prickles of unspoken bruised feelings.

Our group of twelve had been allocated four keys to the shower and toilet block. Tim had decreed that they would permanently reside on the finial of his tent pole unless actually being used to gain access to these facilities. Thus, in the unlikely event of no keys being present there, it must follow that four of us had independently needed to use them and that the fifth would just wait upon someone's return, and not need to forage round the camp to see who had a key.

I was up first the following morning. I knew that we were not going to get the show on the road particularly early – nor was there a need to – but it seemed sensible to start the long wind up through morning ablutions, breakfast, tidying the camp, preparing packed lunches and filling rucksacks as soon as possible. There would also need to be a briefing meeting for the whole team before departure to describe the plan and ensure that all emergency procedures were fully understood, as well as to encourage members to keep within sight of one another and agree any side excursions with 'the leadership'.

There was only one key on the finial. Nothing in the camp stirred. Could I complete my morning routines and get the key back before anybody else arose? It would undoubtedly be Tim – he was not one for lying abed while the morning glowed around him. There could be a serious diplomatic incident – three keys were lying in others' pockets, by sleeping bodies, in clear contravention of camp rules. No I couldn't. The incident was already in progress on my return. But at least it got the team on the move earlier that might otherwise have been possible!

The day before had been cold and I advised the adventurers to take their warm clothing. In fact this proved quite unnecess-ary, as this day of the climb was both warm and sunny with just a touch of cumulus in the sky to add interest and give a little shade from time to time. One thing the Australians are exceptionally good at is avoiding the perils of sunburn, and we learnt a great deal from them here, applying various scented and viscous liquids to those parts of our anatomies where the sun rarely reaches in our climate.

The route took us through the headwaters of the Snowy River – of interest to the Australians largely by association with the film about the man therefrom and its music. Their knowledge of their own country's geography was on a par with that of the night sky and, indeed, most Scots of the geography back home. However, what really made a lasting impression on us was the native reaction to snow, of which there was a great deal lying at these heights, even in midsummer.

It is commonplace to us, and the response of those who have never seen it before, therefore, becomes remarkable. I first met this with a couple of teenage winter visitors to Edinburgh. Their home was in South Africa and they had only ever experienced snow through photographs. Now they could walk in it, feel it, sledge in it, taste it and feel cold. Gérard, also from South Africa, passed his Cairngorm Test on Ben Ledi on Boxing Day, 1997. On that occasion we were offered the full treatment, and he was by no means disappointed! Now one of our great joys in taking those brought up in hot climates on winter excursions is to witness the simple pleasure they derive from experiencing snow for the first time.

On Kosciusko I was besieged with requests to divert to it and these could reasonably be denied as there would be more later, right on our path. Our boys taught the Australians how to make snowballs. They learnt quickly and seemed to be giving as good as they got in the ensuing fights. 'The leadership' managed to keep well clear of these activities!

At the top only two of the junior members showed any enthusiasm for the longer ridge walk home, and these were soon persuaded by some of their elders that the bar at Charlotte's Pass Hotel might be a more welcome alternative and would already be open by the time that those taking the direct return arrived. Thus I had no takers and, feeling that it would be wrong to detach myself alone from the rest of the team, joined them in the walk back and the sampling of the local ale – more than welcome after our day's endeavours.

Thus my grand plan to walk the whole Australian 7,000′ plateau was shelved, to be dusted down later for use on some future visit. An opportunity to do this occurred exactly two years later when we visited our expanding family yet again for Christmas. The other team members had warm memories of their earlier visit to the Snowy Mountains, but were quite happy to let me do the return trip unaccompanied – not quite Ramshead Revisited, as it were. Thus it was that Hazel and I arrived to take up lodgings in Thredbo Village, my plan being to climb under the chairlift early the next morning, use the walkway for rapid access to Rawson's Pass and then spend the rest of a quite leisurely day picking off those peaks that I had missed two years earlier. But it was not to be.

The Australian midsummer mountain weather was atrocious and not forecast to improve for several days yet. However, in the usual spirit of these things, I would start bravely and undaunted. The cloud base was at about 1,600m and the valley below was soon out of sight. The chairlift was not operating at that early time of the morning but by the time I reached the top of its run there were maintenance men in attendance preparing it for the daily opening. They were well insulated against the constant and heavy rain, which seems much more determined there than anything we are used to in Scotland, and expressed incredulity and concern at my activities. I reassured them on the basis that it was just like home.

The Australians are trying to make their ski resorts all year round attractions and, as well as offering lifts into the mountains for casual walkers, there are a number of family facilities at ground level. This has the disadvantage for us climbers that there are no reduced summer rates for accommodation although, in the week before Christmas, with very little demand, we were able to arrange a more than reasonable package.

With the walkway leading me through the fog to exactly where I needed to be, I could dispense with map and compass for this part of the journey. Even in those conditions the pass looked familiar and I soon found the start of the ridge walk, heading off north from Kosciusko's flank.

There was thunder in the distance now, and then more lightning. I would count the five-second intervals to see how far away the centre of the storm was. Then a blinding flash, more intense than anything I had experienced before, with Thor's great explosion following without measurable interval. Time to curl up like a very wet hedgehog and wait – and pray. I found myself wondering if the insurance company would

TIME TO CURL UP LIKE A VERY WET HEDGEHOG

accept a pair of charred boots salvaged from somewhere near the source of the Snowy River, New South Wales, Australia as evidence of my demise, or if Hazel would be in some difficulty claiming her inheritance. I was also extremely grateful to be off the metal walkway!

The path was quite difficult to discern over snow and through boulder fields, and it did not follow the ridge exactly, preferring to sidestep various minor peaks along the way, Mount Northcote in particular. Thus my navigational skills were fully tested in an environment where magnetic and grid north have a very different relationship from that prevailing in the UK.

For a brief but magical twenty minutes the clouds lifted just
enough to afford me a view down to Lake Albina, and the
sensation of being in the Cairngorms, which Andrew and I had
first experienced on our earlier visit, returned. I could almost
persuade myself that I was standing on Carn Etchachan looking
down into Loch Avon. But it was soon over. The cloud thick-
ened, the sleet increased in intensity, and I set off again, head
down, into the blustering storm.

From the top of Carruthers Peak I would have to make the
traverse to Mount Twynam and its outliers, the northernmost
sentinels of the plateau. Decision time. I turned back. If the
rain abated by the time I returned to Mueller's Pass, I could
then do the side trip north-west to Mount Townsend and its
associated peaks. (This had appeared on my previous trip to be
the most challenging section of the route and would best be
covered in clear visibility.) If it did not then the decision to turn
back would not have cost me anything in the way of views or
exhilaration other than the continual struggle against wind and
rain.

However, there was no respite from the foul weather and now
there were further sounds of thunder in the distance. I returned
to Rawson's Pass and met the only other people I had seen all
day since leaving the chairlift's upper terminus. It was mid-
afternoon and they decided to struggle on for a while just in
case the weather improved. It didn't.

Nor was the next day any more promising. We returned to
Melbourne for the family Christmas festivities. The Australian
7,000′ plateau remains to be finished.

All the 7,000′ peaks in Australia lie in this section of the Great
Dividing Range, with only ten miles of undulating high-level
walking separating Mount Twynam from Ramshead in the
south. At no point does the plateau drop below 2,000m, including the western extension to the Mount Townsend group.
I believe it could be fully covered in a single strenuous day, and

look forward to putting this to the test on some future visit to that beautiful country when, perhaps, the weather will be kinder.

There are twelve distinct summits – in the sense of Munro – and I shall refer to them as the Australian Super-Munros, or SAMs for short – it makes a better acronym. Here then is my suggested Section 18 of the Tables (Australia – 7,000′ summits) as Munro himself might have proposed it:

SAM Name	Height	No. in Order of Altitude Mtn. Top		Map Sheet CMA	Map Reference
				8525	FV
1. Mount Kosciusko	2,228	1	1	II & III	131645
2. Mount Townsend	2,209	2	2		127683
3. Alice Rawson Peak – North Top	2,160		8		132690
4. Mount Twynam	2,196	3	3		178715
5. Watsons Crags	2,136		12		165717
6. Ramshead	2,190	4	4		127607
7. North Ramshead	2,177		6		136616
8. Central Ramshead	2,175		7		130611
9. Mount Etheridge	2,180	5	5		139643
10. Abbott Peak – SW Top	2,159	6	9		117675
11. Abbott Peak	2,145		10=		122677
12. Carruthers Peak	2,145	7	10=		156696

There is a degree of inconsistency among the various maps I have used, both as to nomenclature and numerics, and these heights have been taken from the book *Snowy Mountain Walks*, Seventh Edition, published in 1991 by the Geehi Bushwalking Club. This notes 'that some of these heights are estimated'. My SAM Section may, therefore, bear some future revision when further and better particulars become available, not unlike Munro's Tables themselves! Perhaps Mount Etheridge should be reclassified as a Top of Mount Kosciusko – there is not quite 250' of fall.

You don't have to go a great deal further than this to cover all the 6,000' peaks in Australia – the Double Munros? – but you certainly won't manage all these in one day!

New Zealand is yet another story, and I certainly have Mount Cook pencilled in for some future, as yet unplanned, visit. This, of course, will be a different story from that of the simple slopes of Kosciusko.

CHAPTER XI

Why Do Men Climb Mountains?

I was about nine or ten years old when first confronted by this question. It was asked by my then headmistress, a re-markable lady who seemed larger than life at the time but who, like so many memories from childhood, was reduced to a more human scale when I met her again in my own maturity. The question was asked in that form exactly; no doubt in those pre-feminist days she considered such activities unsuitable for women, or that they would not be interested in doing them anyway.

In retrospect I think that her asking the question was prompted by the first conquest of Everest by Hillary and Tensing, admir-ation for which and whom stirred something in her magnificent bosom. Although my classmates and I were really too young to understand these things – that is, magnificent bosoms and the motivation for climbing Everest – there is no doubt that the former, which preceded her into the classroom by at least five minutes, was well noted while the latter became the subject of that evening's homework essay.

The honest answer then was 'I don't know why men climb mountains' but the two sides of quarto duly had to be filled. Whatever I wrote was obviously to her satisfaction since I am still here to tell the tale! Undoubtedly it would have been a load of contrived rubbish – now, nearly two generations on, here is my second attempt at providing some insight.

The answers are far from straightforward, touching, as they

do, some of the deepest human motivations, and I will open the discussion by considering an incident which occurred in Glen Shiel. Andrew and I had been engaged in some rumbustious intercourse with one of the Five Sisters and were back at the car in the lay-by reviewing the damage she had wrought to our feet, peeling off soggy boots and mangled socks matted with various bits of blood, skin and blister.

Suddenly there roared up a hired mini-car which screeched to a halt in front of us, parked at a 45° angle. Out poured four Japanese tourists dressed impeccably in dark business suits, who left all car doors wide open as they pointed animatedly and excitedly towards the somewhat insignificant burn which tumbled down the hillside and which, given the constant rain which had accompanied our earlier encounter with the good lady, could almost be described as being in spate.

The qualities of this experience were being loudly applauded in fast-spoken, high-pitched Japanese while four video cameras comprehensively recorded the tumbling stream. Just as quickly, on some unuttered cue, they piled back into the mini which screamed off and was soon out of sight. The complete event lasted no more than thirty seconds. We didn't have the slightest chance of telling them where the really photogenic opportunities lay, and doubted that they would have been willing to risk scaffing highly polished shoes even if they had been prepared to make the time available.

This incident has prompted me to become a fascinated observer of hom. sap. videoensis at work, and I have reached the following conclusions.

Firstly, the mechanics, electronics and techniques of the video process itself are of much greater importance than the object being recorded. Its precise location in the viewfinder, the correct angle of this to the body of the apparatus, the focusing, the proper direction for the microphone, the adjustments for light quality, the grip on the body itself, the sufficiency of the remaining battery power are all minutely considered, reviewed and adjusted, no doubt with consummate skill, before any images are committed to the magnetic medium.

Secondly, the object itself is seen only in a very generalized way. It is a shape which fits into an equally generalized architectural or pastoral context, the details of which will be elucidated later. It is sufficient at this stage simply to ensure that the procedures outlined in the first priority will suffice to render an image satisfactory in the user's estimation, at the point of commitment. There is no time for more; the next attraction awaits.

Thirdly, it is only in the home surroundings and with benefit of the electronic screen that the videoed image is minutely and repeatedly observed. At this point, and provided that the matters detailed in the first two priorities have been properly attended to, the neo-classical detail, for example, of the National Gallery can be marvelled at for the first time.

Some ten miles from the South Rim of the Grand Canyon there is a cinema where, for a smallish fistful of dollars, you can lay claim to the 'Total Canyon Experience'. All the latest in 3-D film technology is on offer. You can experience a flight down, across and into the Canyon. In air-conditioned luxury you can visit the boiling rapids, treacherous whirlpools and tumbling cascades of the Rio Colorado. Many Americans prefer it this way – to them it is a more valid and complete experience than suffering the heat of the day and feeling the aching tiredness of exhausted limbs. They will settle for this, supplemented by a view over the rim from one of the car parks, preferably at sunset. And where America is today, you can bet that we won't be too far behind.

All of which has prompted me to design a grand master plan for the future of tourism in Scotland – hill-walking and mountain climbing in particular.

We are on the brink of virtual reality. Billions of dollars, pounds sterling and yen are being invested in technology which will make today's videos seem like Victorian epidiascope slides. Interactive video-on-demand over the Internet is where it's at! You can have instant experience in your own home with minimum inconvenience – totally in harmony with modern, thrill-demanding, restless, plastic society.

Each Munro and Top will be comprehensively encapsulated by the best video photographers. Quality will not be compromised. Every starting point, all routes to the summit, each ridge and gully, every corrie from all possible aspects will be committed, digitally of course, for posterity. Each mountain will be offered to the home viewer on a master menu screen. Once he has made his choice the whole video will be downloaded into his PC and he may now begin his virtual ascent. Imagine he has selected Ben Cruachan.

How shall we start? Not done this one before – let's choose an easy route. How about starting from the dam? Then what? Meall Cuanail first, perhaps. We can then go straight for the highest Munro itself and skip the rest until we've had more experience. Look at the views! What's that over there? Computer answer: Ben More on Mull. Wow! Where's Ben Nevis? Computer answer: You can't see it from here – try Buachaille Etive Mor. Booa-what? Computer answer: The Great Herdsman of Etive, one of the best rock climbs in Scotland – but don't go on the north face until you've had a lot more experience.

Let's start again. How about the track up the side of Loch Etive as far as Glen Noe and then climb the mountain from the west – there are no paths there, it'll be more exciting. No, I want to do it from Dalmally – my friend says it's best to walk towards the west as the views are more spectacular.

But so far all our climbing has been in fine weather. Let's ask the computer to include a storm now, so that we can have the virtual experience of being soaked. No, I prefer to keep virtually dry and, anyway, we won't get the views if the weather's bad. But the waterfalls will be torrential – look, I can select for one day's, three days', or a week's rain and we can also choose our virtual season as spring, so that we see the effect of all that melting snow.

The user of these facilities will be electronically billed at a price approximating to 50% of the actual cost of the climb chosen, had he really done it. This will be calculated on the basis of his never needing to buy boots, clothes, maps, tents, sleeping bags, cooking stoves, other equipment, or a mountain bike, and supplemented by a figure to cover his petrol for the journey, a portion of his fixed motoring costs, food and drink, and overnight accommodation if the chosen climb is more than a given mileage from home.

English residents would be given a 10% discount on the journey and accommodation components to encourage virtual tourism by our southern neighbours.

Members of bona fide virtual climbing clubs would be given a 10% discount on the total cost.

There would be rebates for multiple climbs of the most popular mountains – for example, five different ascents of Schiehallion for the price of four.

Certain routes such as the north face of Ben Nevis or the Aonach Eagach would only be available via specially coded 0890 numbers. For an additional premium they would offer the experience of a virtual fall and stretcher recovery by a virtual mountain rescue team using a virtual helicopter.

Who will be the first virtual munroist? Will this accolade be claimed before the millennium? What will be his time? I imagine that, with adroit use of the fast forward button, a complete circuit in under twenty-four hours should be possible. The Scottish Mountaineering Club will need to be in a position to adjudicate upon such matters.

In the early years of the scheme a sufficient proportion of the revenues generated would be used to compensate those whose livings depend upon there being real mountaineers – map and book publishers, equipment makers, boot repairers, B&B land-ladies, expensive petrol purveyors in the Highlands and other dislocated tourist interests. I would also hope to see some of the income being applied to repairing the erosion suffered by our more popular real mountains in the last few years.

The scheme is, of course, revolutionary. It will have a substantial and lasting impact on how tourism and travel are done, necessitating fundamental changes to those university degree courses specializing in this discipline. The planning for all this needs to be attended to now; there is not a moment to lose. The first Chair in Virtual Tourism waits to be assigned!

The main advantages of my scheme are these:

Ecological

It is clear that the technology will be expanded to cover tourism generally, and not just in Scotland. Thus the need for tourists physically to travel anywhere will have been completely eliminated, since any world travel experience will be offered to them at home in a quality format and greater depth than is available to them actually doing it, and at half the cost.

The need for road travel will be confined to necessary vehicle movements such as our previously encountered food delivery lorry, and to those young males who like to burn off their excess testosterone at 90 m.p.h. or more up and down our motorways and trunk roads. There will be a corresponding reduction in the consumption of fossil fuels accompanied by a quantum improvement in atmospheric quality.

No further new roads need be built, and the maintenance budget for the existing network could be slashed. This would release funds for, say, better health care and the reduction of poverty worldwide.

As a general economic trend, hardware – motor car and aeroplane building and transport infrastructure, typically – will be replaced by software – the programming required to satisfy a video-hungry consumer base. This will tend to reduce the requirement for hard raw materials and enable us to curb the despoliation and exhaustion of the earth's mineral resources, and hand on a much 'greener' planet to the next generation.

Health of the Nation

Without the need to rush around the globe in ever-decreasing circles, the stress factor in our lives would be substantially reduced. Furthermore, there will be a dramatic decrease in travel-related accidents and injuries.

In order to maintain the physical fitness of a largely screen-addicted population there would be government-sponsored multi-gymnasia in all residential areas. These would absorb some of the economic slack caused by the decline in the motor and aircraft industries until, of course, they are themselves superseded by the virtual multi-gym in the next generation of this technology.

Education

There would be a strong demand for an educated workforce to design, specify and produce the required video software unless, of course, we are happy to cede this function substantially to the Americans, Japanese and Indians. There would be no need now to teach boring old subjects like Arithmetic and English since they will no longer be required. The new icons will be Virtual Experience allied with Media Studies. These will be underpinned by Commmunications Skills, Marketing, Remote Billing and Software Structure.

The new lingua franca will be Internet Pidgin in the American dialect, limited in functionality and totally devoid of beauty, not taught as such, but absorbed into the brain-stream by constant exposure to the messages on the flickering screen. The universality of this medium will be such that existing languages will no longer be used except by a handful of paper-age dinosaurs, who will resist all these modern trends as they desperately cling to the old ways.

Grammar, syntax and literature will die with them – the new idiom will have no need of such complexities and idiosyncracy.

The Real World

This will be left for that very small percentage of us who cannot cope with such rapid speed of change or who prefer the hands-on, real, albeit imperfect, contact with non-virtual reality. This will have the substantial benefit of leaving the real wilderness and access to it to those of you who value that quality of experience as being substantially and significantly better than that of my conjured up, nightmare, virtual space with its dismal and limited engagement of only a few of our five senses.

I can now begin seriously to answer the question 'Why do men (and women) climb mountains?' There are many threads to unravel, and these are some of them.

The Real Experience

It is difficult to avoid cliché, so maybe I shouldn't dwell on the taste of the wind; the freshness of the smell of the rank grass; the audible stillness; the fifty-strong herd of wild deer silhouetted against the darkening ridge; the black, clear lochan 1,000' below; the surging waterfall; the subtle pastel colours of the heathlands; the sounds of the gathering storm, moaning like a hurt companion; the ever-changing effects of light and shade; the sheer quality of the light itself; the utter peace of the inner corrie; the constant rumble of distant cataracts; the cumulative power of nature in the raw; the delicate fragility and intense colours of the mountain flora; the spongy and springy tundra; the ice grottoes in winter; the menacing hovering and mortal stoop of the osprey; or the fragrance of the ice-cold water.

'Is this water safe to drink?' asked an American friend.

'You bet,' said I, 'That's what we make whisky from.' That evening he took an even closer interest in his dram.

But what about the eyebrows iced up in winter; the boulder field on Ben Nevis looking like a builder's yard; the desolation of the Cairngorm plateau; the exquisite shape of a snow-capped pap; the sleek, slender, spiky spires of Skye; the filigree stonework of the Aonach Eagach, matching any mediaeval cathedral tracery in beauty and structure; the battle for survival between the bee and the dragonfly; the sudden and spectacular view over the other side of the mountain; Sgritheall's smooth, spherical corries; the hexagonal symmetry of the basalt pillars on Bidean; being dive-bombed by aggressive tern on the path to Barrisdale, and on the way back; the glistening frog, so nearly flattened by one's advancing boot; the vertiginous and vertical drop of Shelter Stone Crag; the tartan tweed woven into the fabric of the lower slopes in purple, green, yellow and russet autumnal polychrome; the whole term's geography lessons from the summit of Ben Hope; the stone-camouflaged ptarmigan, so well hidden that she decided only at the last minute to divert me away from her four tiny, yellow, fluffy chicks; the sensuous snow sculptures of Slioch; the gentle gentian of the high alp; most of the population of Deeside sunning itself on the granite tor of Lochnagar, looking from afar as if clinging to it like a colony of bats; the clouds

The sleek, slender, spiky spires of Skye – the northern Cuillin.

being formed high up in a corrie on Ben Vorlich, whipped into shape like celestial candyfloss; the dewy crystal chandelier spiders' webs scintillating in the sunrise; the distant view of the main Cuillin ridge from Loch Hourn, with everything from Gars-bheinn to Sgurr nan Gillean accounted for, including the Inaccessible Pinnacle in silhouette; and the immensity of Ben Avon and its outliers?

And, of course, I must add the cliché of the whole experience being more than the sum of its parts; scenic beauty so special and singular that it brings tears to the eyes.

It is simplistic to talk of an escape from the problems which beset one in daily life, for the mountain wilderness experience is much more than this. It offers a perspective – a more or less absolute frame of reference – for viewing the world. A means of attributing relative importance to life's major and minor decisions. Real peace and quiet. You are required to slow down to the unyielding pace of the wild and, thereby, will achieve a more profound relationship with it, and a greater understanding of your own part in the world at large. The inner satisfaction will enliven and enrich you more surely than any virtual, vicarious experience.

It is difficult to communicate the sheer quality of this to the non-believer, but I think you will know what I am on about – you wouldn't be reading the book otherwise.

This is reality. It is light years away from that ghastly virtual world which I have held up and mocked. It is human sensibility and sensitivity at its quintessential best, untarnished by mediocrity, baseness, or temptation. It transcends the daily grind. It offers hope and consolation. It tells us that we haven't yet quite lost our innocence, and that we can still assure the future as long as such conditions continue to exist and there are sufficient of us to understand the difference.

Thus my first reason for climbing mountains may be summarized as: 'Because it puts us back into contact with our natural

state, both physically and metaphorically'. It unclutters the
mind, frees the spirit and makes the soul soar. Folk ask, 'Do
you climb to get away from it all?' My standard answer now is,
'No, to get back to it all.' Here are some of the other reasons.

Participatory Sport

Those who enjoy hard physical exercise will need no further
encouragement from me. There are contrasts between hill-walking and mountain climbing, on the one hand, and other sports,
however, all of which add up to an experience different in quality
and in kind. Here are some:

* There is no set circuit, you make your own.

* There are no set start and finish times, you make your own.

* There are few records to beat unless you are keen, say, to
  climb all the Munros in a shorter time span than has been
  achieved by anybody else, and you will, therefore, set your
  own standards.

* You can be successful without investing expensively in
  equipment or facilities.

* You can do it in all weathers anywhere in the world.

* You can do it alone or in company.

* You can derive total satisfaction even after completely failing
  to meet your planned objectives, which will remain as a
  possible future challenge until the end of your life or the next
  ice age, whichever event occurs first.

* You can accept increasingly more demanding challenges as
  your experience and capabilities develop.

* The possibilities are limitless.

❊ You will be doing something at some time that nobody else has ever done before in quite the same way.

❊ You will see and discover things unknown hitherto to anybody else.

Over a period of prolonged application you will develop a state of mountain fitness in which you will transcend the pain and feel that you could go on for ever. I have only experienced this two or three times in my campaign and was at first quite suspicious of it. I have not, therefore, been able to put it to an objective test. There is no doubt, however, that such a euphoric state can exist and that, perhaps, it represents the ultimate achievement.

I am also in no doubt now that our sport is addictive. Consider the tragic list of well-known climbers who have lost their lives in recent accidents. They had already achieved infinitely more than a mere mam will ever accomplish. Yet they still went on. There is always a beyond. Why?

This is something you must take seriously. There has to be an escape route if it starts becoming compulsive. Take up golf – it's a lot safer!

There is a dark side to what I am encouraging you to do which I don't fully understand, and which frightens me when I start thinking about it. The pull is always there. My inevitable antidote is to lead a very busy life – at the moment – which limits the frequency of excursion. But what will happen when the busyness begins to subside? At the time of writing this I reckon to need another two years to finish the job. Today I set completion as my final objective. Any further climbing will be casual, perhaps with young friends to show them the way, without pressure of strenuous targets, a pain-free exploration of other parts of Scotland and the world, low-level walks in which Hazel will be happy to participate – whatever is required to wind down the outward and upward urge.

Geographical Awareness

I was climbing Beinn Chabhair from Glen Falloch and this huge mountain appeared in the west over the ridge opposite, growing more and more enormous as I went higher and higher. What on earth was it? The only Munro in that direction was Beinn Bhuidhe and it was much further away and didn't look at all like that.

In fact it was Ben Lui, confirmed by a consultation with the map. In my mind's eye the road up the west side of Loch Lomond and through Glen Falloch, taking in Crianlarich and then up Strath Fillan, pointed due north. But there is a dog leg at Crianlarich and the stretch I was overlooking actually runs north-east. Ben Lui had been rotated in my mind some 45° from its true position.

Coming south over Slochd Summit there is a magnificent range of hills to your right. What are they? There's nothing of that scope and complexity over there. They are, of course, the Cairngorms to the south. The road runs east for that short stretch but the mind associates right with west.

I have usually approached the Glen Affric area from Inverness or Drumnadrochit and it is, therefore, always associated with the east of Scotland. It came as a considerable surprise, therefore, on an early visit to Glen Shiel to find it over there in the west also.

These apparent enigmas test one's understanding of the geography of Scotland, particularly in those areas where no roads run and which might otherwise remain unvisited. There is no doubt that mountaineers know far more about our country than others, and even those who do no more than the West Highland Way return home with a much improved sense of what's where.

I doubt if this is sufficient reason on its own for setting off, but it does represent a substantial bonus.

As an exercise I recommend that whenever you reach the top

of anything and have a view, you try and name everything you can see – other peaks, lochs and lochans, rivers, roads and centres of habitation – at first without looking at the map. You will soon become adept at this. It is only then that the relationships between, say, the Glen Shiel hills and the rough bounds of Knoydart become clear.

As your campaign progresses you will begin to find that you have already climbed many of those in your sights, and the whole exercise becomes quite simple and most enjoyable. However, there will usually be something in the distance, off the map, which will frustrate you on the journey home until wider reference is available to reveal the blindingly obvious!

There are two other matters worth noting here. I find it extremely difficult to estimate relative height between or among adjacent peaks. As you move towards, around or away from them, their disposition will seem to change. During the ascent the perception of where the summit actually sits is subject to constant revision unless you are on one of those hills where this is clear right from the start. Even at the top, other nearby bumps can look higher.

After walking the Grey Corries' ridge I did an exercise during my descent on the Glen Spean side to try and identify the exact position of each Munro and Top. Perhaps you will be more successful!

All of this means, of course, that estimates of time and distance made in the field may need to be reviewed from time to time as the true topology unfolds.

Secondly, I find angular displacement difficult to judge accurately. That is to say, summits which, from your current position, look on the map to be nearly in a straight line, for example, and are set wider apart than you may think. This may be just a personal foible. You can put it to the test like this. In your home town, which you will know quite well, go to a viewpoint – maybe your office or a window at home will be appropriate – and try and identify every tall building on your horizon – church spire, town hall, broadcasting mast, castle or hill, with and without a map. See what I mean?

Character Building

I have mixed views about this.

As a mam, your character will already be built. It will be this character which drives you forward into the hills, and not the being in the hills which moulds your character. What about the young, though?

There is no doubt that the 'Outward Bound' type of experience is helpful in many different ways. I am not so sure about rugged exposure as an instrument of reformation, however. The 'short, sharp shock' philosophy seems an over-simplistic cure for the range of ills for which it is sometimes proposed.

Nor am I convinced that leadership qualities are born in the hills. Certain aspects may be honed there; the basic ingredient, however, comes separately packaged, like blue eyes or a balding pate. You've either got it or you haven't.

There are those who assure me that executives or politicians are improved by a course of survival in the wilderness. It's certainly plausible. But will they learn anything new about themselves? If so, will they be able to apply it effectively on coming back down to earth? Can we look forward to an improvement in the quality of government as a result? It's an intriguing thought!

However, it seems unlikely that if you were to put 600-odd MPs down at the start of a mountain climb they would ever be able to agree on a way forward. And as an aside, any of my readers who cling to the notion that punctuation is of no importance may like to consider the effect of removing the hyphen from that last sentence. As for 600-odd civil servants, the route would have been subjected to heavy rock falls or become densely afforested by the time they had agreed and completed all the right procedures.

What is clear, though, is that the mountain experience is a sterling test of determination. Richard is a frequent visitor and was often badgering me to give him a Munro. Our first outing together was to Beinn Eunaich with Beinn a' Chochuill as an optional extra, to be included if we did particularly well. Within ten minutes of leaving the path he wanted out. He was quite happy to wait back in the car while I finished the job.

On a later visit he asked to go again. This time he was ready. I took him up Sgorr Dhonuill on Beinn a' Bheithir. It was absolutely clear that he was going to succeed, whatever the cost. The will to overcome was palpable, measurable even. We did it. He was not interested in the traverse to Sgorr Dhearg; he had met his personal target of climbing a Munro.

On visits now he quite happily accompanies me up the first peak or two, returns to the car by his own route and collects me later in the day at the end of some long traverse. It works well for both of us.

What was impressive was the summoning up of the will and strength to do it after discovering how far short he fell at the first attempt. This was latent in his character – the mountain didn't put it there.

I have seen the same response in youngsters who suddenly find out how much more is expected of them than they ever conceived, and how they can then respond magnificently to the challenge.

There is also the related matter of confronting danger, and this may be one of the addictive ingredients. You will know how far you are prepared to go in this department, the further as your technical skills develop. Risk analysis will set the exposure into an organized frame of reference so that you do not go beyond known limits – until the unexpected happens. Then you will come face to face with fear, and maybe it is this element which will make the most significant contribution to any character formation. This is also addictive!

Companionship

I have already noted the pleasure to be derived from meeting fellow walkers and climbers engaged in pursuing similar goals. There is an immediate communion. Furthermore, you are meeting some of the world's true individuals – those who are not afraid to devise their own way of doing things rather than follow set norms – and a fascinating experience this can be.

There is always something to learn from spending a few moments talking to such people, even if it is simply that one of you is going the wrong way!

However, the companionship of someone known to you, friend or family, is greatly deepened by these journeys into the unknown. There are shared trials and dangers to be confronted and overcome, shared experiences to savour, and then there are the close bonds which develop within any group in which collective safety is so much the responsibility of each individual. In the mountains you will meet the real person, not the carefully presented product normally paraded for public view.

I am not so certain about the companionship of dogs, however. In the mountains they seem to me to introduce an unwelcome whiff of domesticity, and they are rarely well controlled.

I remember an occasion when I was rejoining the main path down Lochnagar after a cross-country traverse from Meall Coire na Saobhaidhe. There was a herd of a hundred or so deer in the corrie, just out of sight of the track. A woman and her dog, running anywhere it might, passed me going up. I warned her of the danger and heard more well-spoken expletives and assorted swear words in those few seconds than in any other similar short period of my life to date.

Some dog owners are strange folk; incomprehensible to us who inhabit canine-free areas.

And yes, I have met the good lady who habitually walks her hound up and down Schiehallion (all the way, every day?). In the final analysis, I suppose, we must rejoice in a world that breeds such eccentricity!

But there is another reason, deeper and much more difficult to put into words. It is the most profound reason of all and I have, therefore, put it into a chapter by itself. It is so out of tune with our earlier virtual world as to be unrecognisable from it. I will call it the spiritual dimension.

THE GOOD LADY WHO HABITUALLY WALKS HER

HOUND UP AND DOWN SCHIEHALLION

CHAPTER XII

The Spiritual Dimension

I was baptized an Anglican but my parents converted to Roman Catholicism when I was about four years old and, not unnaturally, took me with them. Thus my school education, as required by that religion, was in the hands of nuns, priests, and committed Catholic laity.

At a very young age we were taught – with the full weight of Roman Authority, and that is some weight – that only Catholics would go to Heaven. There were other places reserved for 'the separated brethren', not least, The Other Place. None of my close relatives – aunts, uncles, cousins, grandparents – was a Roman Catholic, indeed, I believe my parents' conversion/defection (I am not particularly fussed about which word you might prefer) caused a certain amount of rumbling within the wider family. This edict, therefore, came as bad news. My archetypal, silver-haired, saintly gran not in Heaven? No chance!

Fortunately I was blessed with enough good sense not to take that statement too seriously, and my parents valiantly attempted to soothe any doubts with emollient balm – 'Perhaps you didn't quite hear it properly, dear?' But I was there and they weren't, and I know what I heard.

This early scepticism coloured my total approach to the evaluation of Roman Catholic doctrine. However, there was no opportunity to consider alternatives. Attempted control was total. Any participation in other religious practices would occasion the state of Mortal Sin – a one-way, non-stop ticket to

That Other Place unless, of course, you could obtain absolution by confession, and that was in the gift of the clergy. Even to enter a church building of another denomination was to tempt Providence. It might be alright if you were a brass-rubber or had some special interest in Victorian stained glass which could not otherwise be satisfied, but it may be as well to seek the Bishop's permission first . . .

One teenage incident stands out clearly in my mind. During school holidays I had slipped into a local Anglican Church to find out for myself. All I had to go on was rumour, and most of that was pretty discreditable. Long before the word ecumenical became common currency I was sitting in an Anglican pew praying for just such reconciliation, and that what I was doing was not going to earn me a place in Hell. I kept this so secret, telling nobody, least of all parents or school authorities, and only some time later managed to get it into a proper perspective in my own mind. Now it amuses me to be disclosing it in a public document. I returned to that church recently, now locked throughout the week to protect it from vandalism, and offered a similar prayer from its churchyard.

I think that the beginning of the end of my involvement with Rome came when a full understanding of that Church's treatment of Galileo finally became clear. 'It was not so much that Galileo was right or wrong,' intoned the priest who taught me Physics – and a superb teacher he was, too – 'but the manner in which he made public his discovery.' So, finally, this from a Prince of that Church which throughout my formative years had justified itself as being the only source of Absolute and Objective Truth. It took the art of information management as seriously as did any totalitarian state; Truth took a back seat.

What became clear later was that the Church of Rome, indeed, any Church, is simply an organization, an institution. Organizations and institutions exist primarily to ensure their own preservation and perpetuation. Any declared objectives – service to members or service to the public, for example – are secondary. It's a form of genetic survival at the corporate level.

You may like to consider the following specific examples in the context of your own experience, each of which illustrates the point in a slightly different light – the takeover of a company, the receivership of a company, the disbandment of a regiment, the reorganization of a local authority, the decline of a gentlemen's club through increased costs and the falling away of new membership applications, the union of two churches, or the winding up of a quango, assuming, that is, you can find an example of the latter, for they are the most effective at exhibiting the behaviour I am describing.

Such organizations cannot cope with the Galileos of this world – and I wouldn't necessarily hold universities immune from these strictures. Any piece of really original thinking which might imply radical progress is anathema to them. They are comfortable only with self-controlled change which causes as little disturbance as possible to their establishments. The Galileos will survive without them – thank God – shining lights into dark corners and exposing cant and hypocrisy wherever they meet it, and usually to their own peril.

I have nothing against the Church of Rome or those who find sanctuary within its embrace. However, I do wonder, from time to time, about the wickedness of filling young minds with such nonsense as to condemn their relatives thus, and very much hope that it's not still going on.

One of the more amusing things we were told was that, whereas the Catholic Church teaches that people are definitely in Heaven by declaring them to be Saints, it has no corresponding mechanism for declaring them to be definitely in Hell. Nevertheless, we could be reasonably certain in assuming that Luther would have been sent there! It is now my earnest hope that both Galileo and Luther are together in Heaven, preferably in adjacent Grand Circle seats, for I feel sure that they will have a lot to talk about during the intervals. Certain Princes of the Church who for legal reasons would best remain nameless, I hope to see in limited-view accommodation high up at the back, in the smoking area.

And one final thought on Roman antecedents. A particularly Gothic train of thought insisted that the purpose of life is death. But a great deal of living can be done before that inevitable event. Maybe fellow mams will draw strength from my current view that the purpose of life is life!

Now we are members of the Church of Scotland in our local community. That is to say, I am not a conviction Presbyterian, but feel it is right and proper for church life and work to be done in and around those among whom one dwells, and that it is no longer a matter of this or that denomination – or even world religion or non-religion – being more right than any other. I will happily concede that each has its own insights and none the total answer. I do hope, however, that Heaven is not run by a cacophonous chorus of committees. The notion that Presbyterian Church government is pleasing to God I regard as that church's own Assumption!

What cannot be lost on the objective observer is the extent to which personal faith is so much a matter of cultural formation, for we are all products of our own background and experience. Hardly worth going to war over religious differences, you might agree, but that really is outside the scope of my remit. I have no doubt that, born in the Punjab, I would have been a Himalayan Hindu rather than a Munroving Christian. The search for the ultimate meaning of life and objective truth – even assuming these to be valid concepts – is far too demanding and interesting for any one particular religious, metaphysical or philosophical strain to insist upon exclusive shooting rights over its terrain. And as for the historical perspective, not to say what the future might unfold for us, well, I must now return to the high ground.

We had been up in Glen Affric and I had decided to take the

Sunday off from climbing. Instead we attended the local 11 a.m. morning service. Churches have in common with the railways that they run to a regular timetable and will continue to operate the advertised service even with no passengers. However, this one was well attended.

I was explaining to the Minister that I could be closer to God in the hills than in the pew, and that my original plan for that day had envisaged the former method of worship. He did not, however, share my sense of humour and began lecturing me on the specific and the general experience of God. Some Ministers of Religion are really quite difficult to communicate with!

Not so George. If I slip away on a Sunday morning and tell him that I'm going to visit 121, he knows, of course, that I don't mean the Church of Scotland headquarters in George Street, Edinburgh, but ... well, you'll find it in the Bible!

I have found lifting mine eyes unto the hills to be a deeply spiritual experience. This is not always so, and I have not yet been able unequivocally to identify the conditions under which it will invariably be so, apart from having an open mind. It is certainly true that going into the wilderness features in all religions as bringing the pilgrim into closer communion with his God. That place of retreat is usually stony desert, whereas ours is soft and boggy in its usual state. Whatever its texture, the wilderness is traditionally seen to be a place conducive to spiritual awareness.

One reason is born out of the sheer physical hardship. Not that every visit to the hills is exhausting. But even the simplest summer stroll taxes the body, tires the limbs and requires the ignoring of a degree of pain. The foul weather, wintry, demanding and danger-filled excursions are, of course, of a different order. Both types of experience, however, impose their own demands, and it is in responding to them that the mind is placed in a state more susceptible to the spiritual dimension.

As already hinted, there is, on occasions, the need to overcome fear. Failure to succeed here will lead to panic, poor decision making in the emergency, increased danger and, ultimately, serious injury or even death. We are not now in virtual space where the whole trauma can be wiped away at the touch of a button. This is real. It cannot be coincidence that people return to the Church in times of great crisis or hardship in their lives.

Then there is the sheer beauty and breathtaking wide-openness which we have already discussed, opening the mind to a world apart from the normal daily round.

These thoughts first coalesced in Torridon where the beauty and grandeur are of the highest order. Now you will begin to understand why I have called it God's own country.

Of course, the mechanics of geoformation are accessible to the O grade scientist and, as a scientist of sorts, I approach the matter of belief in God with all the assurance of the sanctity of scientific methodology. However, there is something in Torridon which speaks of other approaches. There is an orderliness to it all; those sandstone terraces are not there by accident; those corries, lochans and straths are not just a by-product of a world-scale cooling down of former stellar material.

The Uncertainty Principle is one of the great pillars of twentieth-century Physics. No reputable scientist since Heisenberg has seriously questioned its validity. The Principle has to do with the amount of knowledge we are able to gather about the universe's goings on. It places limits, both theoretical and practical, upon this knowledge. In simple terms it tells us that it is intrinsic to the nature of matter that we cannot know everything there is to know about it.

I find this deeply satisfying. At a metaphysical level, if we cannot know everything then what can this tell us about the nature of knowing and knowledge? At a religious level, what might it tell us about an all-knowing God?

There are those Ministers who are troubled about a possible conflict between Science and Religion; that the momentous advances of the former will eventually annihilate the latter, demanding, as Science does, validated proof of every conjecture, assertion and theory. This leaves, or so it seems to them, no room for the Act of Faith. No reason to believe in something which cannot be established beyond doubt by humanist analysis. I do sympathize.

This side of the argument was neatly summarized by the Minister of another Highland parish when he told me, 'Science takes the mystery out of Religion.'

I believe that this statement is misguided and pessimistic. It seems to me that in our scientific unravellings of any discipline, be it in molecular biology and genetic engineering, space exploration and observation of remote events, or smashing atoms into even smaller particles, we are simply confirming that our universe is much more complicated than any scientist in history has imagined.

Each big leap – Galileo, Newton, Bohr, Darwin, Franklin – simply takes us further into the unknown. It reveals how little we really understand and how much more remains to be discovered. I believe that this is the proper function for Science and that it will always be so. We will never know it all, and this is an essential part of the human condition, deducible by humanist convention.

Far from destroying Religion, I believe that Science underpins it. It points the need for something other than Science to explain the huge why? that hangs over all of us. If my Minister friend had said, 'Science takes the mythology out of Religion' then I would heartily agree and thoroughly applaud. But do the people who make such statements understand the difference between them? And how does the atheist scientist explain the existence of, say, Bruckner's 'Te Deum'?

These notions may come into full focus in the hills. I believe that one can come to an awareness of a supreme creator out there, and that it is not necessary to be eccentric, demented, a

A fleeting glimpse into the beyond Celtic mist insinuating Celtic
mysticism – Rhum from Skye.

yogi, conditioned by mysticism, or in a state of hallucination to do so. We are still, of course, miles from Atonement or the Trinitarian Deity; these matters can safely be left to the theologians. But it's a useful start.

My erstwhile headmistress answered a fellow callow youth with 'Heaven is within us'. Nearly fifty years further down the line I have to confess little understanding of what she meant. It's either utterly facile or of impossible profundity. She will know now where Heaven is. May she rest in peace.

I find the state of being fogbound on a Highland ridge a most convincing metaphor for the spiritual search. The way forward in any direction is diffuse; the land-shape is ambiguous and difficult to determine; the clouds may part and offer a fleeting glimpse into the beyond, a mere touch of light in the overall gloom; map and compass offer a means of navigation towards righteousness; and the price of failure could be high. The quest for Absolute and Objective Truth becomes synonymous with the search for the Holy Grail – both are equally unattainable.

My own religious position can now quite simply be stated: I am prepared to make a virtue of uncertainty! This means that the neglected and underrated great virtue of Hope replaces the more familiar and overworked one of Faith, leaving Charity available to all on every side of this fascinating debate.

CHAPTER XIII

Decline and Fall

How do I know I'm at the top? I presume that others who write books on hill-walking or climbing find the answer obvious, as I have never seen the matter referred to anywhere else. I do not find it obvious at all, at least, not in every case.

Have a look at the summit plateau of Beinn (not An) Teallach. Which is the geographical top – the large cairn or the small one? Does the map help to elucidate this? If you are wrong and didn't visit both cairns, can you claim to have reached the summit? Have you, therefore, climbed the mountain? Does it matter?

Now consider the summit plateau of Moruisg. There are three cairns there, almost in a straight line, the south-western one having been almost totally demolished at the time of my own visit. Presumably that one may be ruled out as the summit. If you draw an imaginary straight line from there to the north-eastern cairn then the central one would stand proud above it. Provided your line was horizontal, therefore, elementary geometry would indicate this to be the summit. But is it horizontal? Without surveying equipment how can you tell? Just a slight incline upwards towards north-east could put the remoter cairn higher. Do you have any innate, absolute sense of the horizontal? Try the same exercise on Luinne Bheinn.

Drive over Drumochter, or Shap Fell on the M6 and note the signs which identify the summit. Doesn't the road still appear to climb once you've passed them? In either direction! Of course, the surveyors could have got it wrong. In both cases?

If all this still hasn't driven you mad have a look at Tom Dubh in the Cairngorms. There are half a dozen or so individual cairns adorning its summit plateau, which is of undulating, neither convex nor concave topology. Which is the top? From any one some of the others look higher. However, that's to be expected. But there are other points on that plateau which look even higher than any of the cairns. So, how do I know I'm at the top? A page further on and we're no nearer an answer.

So far I'm assuming clear visibility, that you can actually see another cairn from the one you've arrived at. But what if you can't and you have no further information? The map is a help, of course, particularly when you have developed a good sense of the relationship between distance actually travelled in the prevailing conditions and that on the map itself, but not even the larger scale 1:25,000 can resolve the examples I have already given.

Read what M says about Beinn Dorain. I found the cairn after having climbed from Bridge of Orchy on a foul day, with the cloud hovering just above the Beinn Dorain/Beinn an Dothaidh saddle, and turned back immediately to climb the latter before returning to the car. Of course, I should have studied M first, but sometimes it is more fun to have a go without such guidance. Will my claim to munroist status be vitiated by this missing of the true summit? Should I go back and do it again? Is there an answer at all? Perhaps I'll just leave it unclimbed in this sense as an acknowledgement of the vain and abject futility of much human endeavour.

So the question remains: how do I know I'm at the top?

There is a further complication. Some cairns are clearly not at the summit, nor intended to be. Also, not every top is invariably cairned, although these are few and far between. In fine weather there is reasonable certainty. Once on the plateau you can visit all those points about which there is the slightest ambiguity. You will want to do this anyway to take full advantage of the 360° views. In fog, however, more care will be required.

Then there is the matter, previously introduced, of sizing up a snowfield. Even in fine weather it can be difficult to delineate. If it is discontinuous then some idea of its shape and general disposition can be learned. If it is crossed by footprints, these also help to give an idea of its contours. If, however, it is virgin pure, white as far as the eye can see, then it becomes virtually impossible to infer anything about its formation, its inclination to the horizontal, whether it is rounded or flat, and even whether it starts from your present position by rising or falling.

All this means that in snow and fog disorientation can be total. There is no sense of up and down, no distance or perspective, and only the compass offers any contact with the physical world below. This is a profoundly fascinating but also frightening discovery, as those of you who have experienced it will attest.

Fortunately most snowfields are not virgin pure in this sense, and there is usually some feature of landscape available to provide a context for one's position and offer some means of determining whether the way ahead lies up, down or just flat.

Now to answer the question. When I have reached that which purports to be the summit in such conditions, and assuming that the shape of the peak does not unambiguously proclaim this, I begin to explore the plateau systematically for dips and rises and further cairns. It was in doing this at the top of Sron a' Choire Ghairbh that I very nearly brought my own quest for mamhood to a violent and premature end. It was the first of that season's outings with crampons, and I had taken advantage of the snowfields to follow a straight line to the summit from the Meall na Teanga col. There was a fairly thin mist at the top, so that the sun's halo could be discerned, but thick enough not to afford a clear view beyond the cairn apart from the fact that the north side of the mountain was heavily snow-clad, as was to be expected. My search began and I stepped right off into empty space.

There is a surreal quality to the experience of free fall which effects a total detachment from the realities and dangers involved; fortunately it doesn't last for long. Now is the time to learn that using the ice axe to break a slide is different in practice from the mostly forgotten routines perfected too long ago.

Firstly, one didn't seem to be in contact with the ground for long enough to dig the wretched thing in. Secondly, one seemed to be rolled up like a spineless hedgehog and never the right way up to put one's full weight on it even assuming it could have been dug in.

Fortunately it was possible to dig the crampons in, each occasion slowing the rapid rate of acceleration, and each time turning the whole body through an unpredictable angle as its centre of gravity was repositioned in accordance with Newton's simple laws.

Finally it happened. I was on top, with full weight bearing down on the ice axe, and carving a spectacular furrow as, seemingly imperceptibly, I broke the slide. Still at last, squatting precipitously over who knows what? No ice axe. Like the cartoon Tom, of Tom and Jerry, with a halo of starry lights, having been hit over the head with a hammer. The left side felt worst affected and was covered with matted blood and ice. I was alive! Time to take stock.

I had left the rucksack at the cairn before setting off to explore the plateau. Thus there was no map to refer to. I hadn't a clue what lay below and could see nothing through the fog. To go back up would offer the best chance of recovery; any other solution was fraught with danger. I had no idea how far I had fallen but reckoned that it would not have been as far as it felt. At such times in one's life time appears to slow down. I was guessing some 250'–300'.

Bumps and scratches in the ice identified my route of descent; it could now be more or less simply retraced to regain the summit. Thank God for the crampons! The slope felt about 35°–40°, too steep for an unaided ascent in those conditions. About 30′ up, and there was the ice axe, its band wrenched from my arm in the whirlwind action, but having done enough to break the fall and bring me to rest below. Upward progress was painstaking but straightforward. I now had three firm points of contact and a clearly marked route. It was just about half an hour before I saw the cairn again, after a final desperate push back through the hole in the cornice which my downward thrust had punched. What a wonderful moment, and how sweet is life. My legs were trembling with a mixture of shock, fatigue and emotion.

And then, a fateful discovery. I had lost my compass. It usually sits in a trouser pocket and must have fallen out in the tumble. Somewhere down there, down the dreaded north face it would be lying, now totally beyond reach. A moment of panic. To us who live by the compass in the mountains life without one seems impossible. How will I get out of this one? Perhaps my time has come after all. Take time; reflect; there's no hurry; plenty of daylight; I know where I am and how I got here; sit and think; eat and drink.

The weather had not changed; still the same thin mist shrouding the summit; still the sun's halo just visible. It was noon-ish, with the sun in the south. That gave me a direction of sorts. Would my weakened frame take me down? Let's try.

Each forward step became a major victory. Each victory built confidence. The route of descent began to look familiar. Wishful thinking? The sun, my navigator, was still there. Now land and features. Burn and bog. The col way down below, only slightly off course. The col gained with legs still trembling.

My original plan had included Meall na Teanga – could that still be on? In retrospect, what an absurd and idiotic question!

Twenty paces up the other side and the whole body unanimously voted no. Back down to Loch Lochy it would have to be, and as the body unfroze so the blood flowed freely and the pain began to gnaw. Dealing with that filled all the time I now had to wait for Hazel's return so that I could present her with a more cultivated image of only a slightly bruised husband. She soon saw through that charade!

This was the first of three planned days of which the second was to be in the Fannaichs. I had to go. As with all such falls in life, it becomes necessary to return as quickly as possible in order to purge any notions of incapacity or phobia. Besides, the time had been committed and the plans laid. A mere fall was not going to be allowed to change all that. I must have looked a picture of incompetence at the summit of Sgurr Mor, for the team who gained it ahead of me suggested that I might, perhaps, like to join them for the descent. Their well-meant offer was declined.

By the time we returned to Edinburgh, however, my inter-mittent, low-grade back problem had become acute and demanding. On this occasion as on many others Anna, physiotherapist par excellence, put Humpty Dumpty together again.

I don't need to dwell on the lessons to be learned from that near miss. The most fundamental change I instituted was to the planning and preparation procedures. Great attention is now given to those parts of mountains which the outing doesn't plan to visit, just in case there comes about a need to know!

I shall finish this chapter by returning to Beinn Teallach. From its small cairn on a fine day there is a view of the profile of the north face of Sron a' Choire Ghairbh. It falls steeply from the summit, becomes shallower for the same distance and then drops like a stone. I guess that I had stopped on the less steep part of the face. But for the ice axe I would probably not be telling you this story. When I return to complete Meall na

Teanga I shall also revisit the Sron to pay my respects – and have another look.

The former is splendid in views from most of the length of the road up the east side of Loch Lochy but the latter, although a slightly higher companion, hides its summit well. You'll need to be looking south down the Great Glen from around Fort Augustus to get a view of the top of that one. Benign it looks too: hardly one of Scotland's great killer mountains.

CHAPTER XIV

Revelation

I will now describe in some detail and in chronological sequence a number of long walks, many of ten to twelve hours
or so and a few of fourteen, and not previously mentioned, in
which I have combined a number of Munros and Tops in ways
which may not immediately seem obvious. Given these times,
we are clearly not talking about winter climbing, but taking
advantage of our long, late spring, summer and early autumn
evenings to derive the greatest potential from the available
daylight.

Some of these are round trips and others have their finishes
miles away from their starts. These latter, therefore, depend on
there being a willing waiter at the other end or, possibly, on
two teams doing the route from opposite ends and exchanging
car keys in the middle (conceptually, that is, for if each team
carries both sets then they don't actually need to meet). In fact
I have never done this but did consider it for the traverse from
Stob a' Choire Odhair to Ben Starav. This would have involved
Andrew dropping me at one end and driving himself to the
other. We each had a map and compass but when the day came
there was fog from 1,500' up. At his then stage of development
I decided not to expose us to the risk of not meeting and the
burden of wondering if the journey was going alright for the
other. I also feel that the small probability of misadventure in
the car while being driven from one end of the route to the
other with only a single member in each team is one I would

wish to consider very carefully in the overall scheme of risk assessment.

I am not suggesting that you would consider following these routes slavishly, but hope you will want to make your own choices, doing more or less than I did within the constraints of what you know to be possible for yourself. In this spirit I am sometimes being deliberately vague as to the precise co-ordinates of my starting and finishing points in order to encourage you to experiment for yourselves and, perhaps, pioneer different journeys altogether.

Sequence of Summits	The Cairnwell, Carn a' Gheoidh, Carn Bhinnein, An Socach – West Summit, An Socach – East Top, Carn Aosda (4 Munros and 2 Tops).
Time of Year	March.
Start and Finish	Glen Shee Ski Centre.

This is one of three walks I have done without proper maps; a procedure not to be recommended. The best wrought plans can be quickly unravelled by a moment's carelessness, and on all three occasions we made do with improvised sketches based upon M's little diagrams.

The Cairnwell, of course, is a gift – just over half an hour from the main road – but mist at the top did not allow any of the route to be seen. The path off to the north was clear enough, however, and the left turn to take us round the corrie towards Carn nan Sac was successfully navigated. This was the first attempt at a substantial 'own plan' route and Andrew was with me. Our handicap was serious, therefore, and we decided to bypass the Carn and as our first priority seek the bealach, not one of those which in fog declares itself unambiguously even to the intrepid, from which Gheoidh would be gained. The pull up the latter's bland, planar west face was one of those heart-in-the-mouth acts of faith which made the journey seem much longer than its advertised half-mile or so.

Mercifully the fog abated just after we had located the summit. Not only could we now confirm our position, but I could fully triangulate the rest of the route so that the remainder of our passage would be done with total peace of mind.

It is on these occasions that one is reminded that sense of direction is not an absolute gift and, in the mountains, is subjected to the most rigorous assessment. Under the discipline of the compass my initial guess as to what was Carn Bhinnein, our next port of call, turned out to be Carn Mor!

The traverse to An Socach stayed as high as possible in the headwaters of the Baddoch Burn, and that from its east end to Carn Aosda took us just north of Loch Vrotachan up Sron nam Fiadh to avoid losing too much height. By now the fog had descended again and finding the Loch was a moment of great comfort.

The descent from our last Munro was unusual. The gully to the side of the ski tow was packed with snow and made a splendid bobsleigh run. We were back at the car park within ten minutes.

Glen Shee is one of Scotland's great weathersheds. That which you experience going up the way portends absolutely nothing of what's waiting for you on the other side. Blue sky can give way to horizontal sleet or, of course, the other way about. In no other arena of human activity does the 'travelling hopefully' need to be taken so seriously or, indeed, so literally.

The greatest weathershed is, of course, Drumochter. But that's another story!

ONE OF SCOTLAND'S GREAT WEATHERSHEDS

<u>Sequence of Summits</u>	Meall Odhar, Creag Leacach, Creag Leacach – South-west Top, Little Glas Maol, Glas Maol, Druim Mor, Cairn of Claise, Carn an Tuirc (4 Munros and 4 Tops).
<u>Time of Year</u>	March.
<u>Start and Finish</u>	Glen Shee Ski Centre.

This walk also has the advantage of the high starting point, and the finding of Meall Odhar in bad weather is greatly assisted by the varied skiing infrastructure east of the pass.

On the first attempt Andrew and I sat in the car confronting total whiteness, for the fog and snow covered everything. Andrew was not at all well and I was disinclined either to take him or leave him. Thus we drove to Pitlochry via Kindrogan – which Sara had enthused about after a Biology field trip – thinking that if both Andrew and the weather improved we might have a shot at Ben Vrackie. The weather did but Andrew didn't, so we experienced Pitlochry now as tourists rather than climbers. The latter, of course, is a very different matter – one is totally out of key sitting in its elegant and genteel tea rooms after a day's exertion in the mountains.

On this revisit I confronted the same white wall – perhaps it's always like that. 'Give in, go home', impelled the siren voices. 'The weather can only improve,' countered the optimist.

It took just the first 100 yards or so to be faced with the 'something in the boot' problem – see Apocrypha 11 – and it was not going to go away of its own accord. So, off with the gloves and through the usual tiresome routine. Ah, that's what I did with the spare laces!

The finding of the Glas Maol/Creag Leacach saddle from

Meall Odhar in the fog was the first challenge, and I very nearly went over the top. By now the snow was falling heavily and the siren voices persisted, yet again to be banished. However, on the way back towards Glas Maol it stopped and suddenly there was a clear view. Like the prisoners in Fidelio, one came out blinking into the blue sky and blinding sunshine. Never was a transformation more rapid or more stunning. The elegant bulk of Creag Leacach could now be appreciated for the first time and there, steeply below in the Isla catchment, were the slippery, icy, shimmering walls of the Caenlochan Glen.

The spirit pulses at such a change. At Cairn of Claise, however, there was a reversal. During the planning I had bought an option on Tom Buidhe and even harboured thoughts of taking in some of the White Mounth itself. But Tom Buidhe was fast disappearing in a blizzard and with the light failing the four miles out and back had little appeal. The sirens now prevailed.

By the time I was doing the two mile uphill trudge along the roadside back to the car the weather had improved again. It had become a fine spring evening. There weren't many cars on the road – I would say about one every five minutes. First you heard it, then saw it. But there was something else. You smelt it. After eight hours up above breathing the purest and most unpolluted air, here on the ground the difference was both palpable and alarming. An approaching car in that environment declared itself by the smell of its exhaust. In the city we must breathe that all the time and don't even notice.

Sequence of Summits	Ben Starav, Stob Coire Dheirg, Meall Cruidh, Beinn nan Aighenan, Glas Bheinn Mhor (3 Munros and 2 Tops).
Time of Year	April.
Start and Finish	Kinlochetive.

This walk was originally planned to include Stob Coir' an Albannaich and Meall nan Eun, with the return by way of Glen Ceitlein, but the weather turned against us after Beinn nan Aighenan. The going had been much tougher and, therefore, slower than we had budgeted for, and a reworking of the sums at the top of Glas Bheinn Mhor showed that we would possibly run out of daylight. The navigation north-east and east was going to be of above average difficulty anyway in the cloud which now enveloped us, and the low-risk percentage play would be to descend via the Allt nam Meirleach. This we did.

From our chosen starting point Ben Starav is a climb from sea level, like so many of the western Munros, and so one is ascending fully 3,500'. When you get to the top you know the difference! The crossing to Beinn nan Aighenan from Meall Cruidh was best done, we felt, on a northern semicircular route so that very little height would be lost to Glen Hallater. This worked well but I wonder if the common practice of not descending further than necessary between peaks isn't more than counterbalanced by the extra distance walked? The desire not to lose height (or not to climb anything unnecessary in the way) can be pursued to the point of neurosis, and it is as well when planning excursions to keep it in a proper perspective.

The remote hinterland each side of Glen Kinglass is considered by some to be the best scenically in all the Highlands – the quintessential Scottish mountain experience – and is, perhaps, not to be rushed through, consuming as many peaks as daylight and human frailty allow. So that is how I consoled myself after falling short of the original objectives!

Sequence of Summits	Tom Buidhe, Tolmount, Crow Craigies, Craig of Gowal, Broad Cairn, Creag an Dubh-loch, Cairn of Gowal, Cairn Bannoch, Fafernie, Carn an t-Sagairt Mor, Carn an t-Sagairt Beag, Carn a' Coire Boidheach (6 Munros and 6 Tops).
Time of Year	May.
Start	Glen Shee Ski Centre.
Finish	Glen Callater.

This return to Glen Shee proved finally that the white wall of previous experience was not a permanent institution after all. That day was to be savoured, not least because Hazel had journeyed with me as far as Meall Odhar. This was her first Top, and the only one to date, so it gets a special pin on the map at home which records these matters. I hope it won't be her last, but she hasn't subsequently said anything which gives me to believe that there will be any more! She did, however, enjoy the nine miles to and from the Falls of Glomach on another occasion except for, as she succinctly puts it, 'That bloody awful Highland weather'.

The fast ascent from the car park leaves the whole White Mounth plateau available, with hardly anything there that is as strenuous as a climb except, possibly, the pull to the top of Carn an t-Sagairt Beag towards the end of the day on tired limbs.

However, there are some spectacular views. That from Tom Buidhe down into Glen Doll, following the line of Jock's Road, is splendid, with Mayar and Driesh beckoning to the right.

Those down to Loch Muick from all round the rim of the Dubh Loch are even more so, and the latter has an enticing sandy beach at the inflow which was utterly deserted. Lochnagar is always impressive, and the view of Loch nan Eun from The Stuic well worth the short diversion.

On this day one could have walked for ever, but for the dehydration. I hadn't carried enough liquid and there wasn't much water that looked at all attractive on that high plateau. Otherwise Creag a' Ghlas-uillt and the Top of Eagle's Rock would have been included, and maybe even Lochnagar itself.

Hazel with the flask was a most welcome sight at Loch Callater.

Sequence of Summits	Beinn Ghlas, Ben Lawers, Creag an Fhithich, An Stuc, Meall Garbh, Meall a' Choire Leith, Meall Corranaich (5 Munros and 2 Tops, or 6 and 1 based upon the 1997 Tables).
Time of Year	May.
Start and Finish	Ben Lawers Information Centre.

If you want to cover the whole Lawers Group in a single outing it is best to traverse from the Loch Tay side to Glen Lyon or vice versa. Meall Greigh is sufficiently detached to the east to make the round trip from the Visitor (sic) Centre or, indeed, anywhere else, anything other than an unmitigated slog.

I digress to mourn the passing of the apostrophe from public usage. Clearly the author lacks the confidence and understanding of our language to commit himself whole-heartedly to 'Visitors' Centre'. You will have your own favourite examples of the misuse of this appendage; here are some of mine: Patients Entrance, Chief Executives Department, Potatoe's 20p/lb. (neatly offering two peccadillos for the price of one!), Passenger's Charter, Doctor's only to park here, Companies House, Mens Haircut's, No person's under 18 admitted. The possible restoration of 'whom' to our language is yet another vain hope.

The key to the above route is the due grid-west traverse from the An Stuc/Meall Garbh saddle to the top of Coire Liath. This involves descending to 1,600' to cross the Allt a' Chobhair and, therefore, takes you almost back to your day's starting altitude.

There are many different ways of approaching these magnificent mountains and dividing them up into individual walks for various times and seasons. The notion of rushing round them just to get the job done, as it were, has little appeal for me, as

I hope I have already made clear, and the opportunity to see the eastern corries overlooking the secretive Lochan nan Cat during winter should not be dismissed lightly. This side of the mountain is very different from that given to the tourist approaching from the south-west, and is something to be savoured at length.

Ben Lawers is, of course, the tallest thing in the British Isles outside the Cairngorms or the Nevis Range. The first view of it when driving north from Glen Ogle is one of Scotland's great images; its singularity confers a status not shared by any of the taller peaks.

And finally, a word about An Stuc. As has already been mentioned, this is steep. It may be the steepest hill you will ever climb. The path is good, but take care!

Sequence of Summits	Beinn Heasgarnich, Creag Mhor, Stob nan Clach, Ben Challum, Ben Challum – South Top (3 Munros and 2 Tops).
Time of Year	June.
Start	Glen Lochay.
Finish	Upper Tyndrum Station.

The main excitement of this walk revolves around how best to deal with Cam Chreag. Avoiding it altogether loses a lot of height to the Allt Challum and leaves you looking at the dauntingly steep north face of Ben Challum itself. I decided to climb over the Chreag at the saddle in the centre of its mile-long ridge and descend from there to the Bealach Ghlas Leathaid. This worked well, but the final pull up Ben Challum was heavy going on a hot summer's day with not enough drinkable water.

The views north and north-west on this concatenation of ridge walks are quite splendid, these relatively higher Munros making hills such as Beinn Mhanach seem of little consequence. That notion is, of course, totally dispelled when you come to climb them!

I would not want to be finding the summit of Beinn Heasgarnich approaching from the east in fog. The topography is complex, and the best method would seem to be the exact following of an accurately set compass.

Sequence of Summits	An Gearanach, An Garbhanach, Stob Coire a' Chairn, Am Bodach, Sgor an Iubhair, Stob Choire a' Mhail, Sgurr a' Mhaim, Stob Ban, Mullach nan Coirean – South-east Top, Mullach nan Coirean (7 Munros and 3 Tops, or 6 and 4 based upon the 1997 Tables).
Time of Year	October.
Start and Finish	Glen Nevis car park.

The first and, for me, principal challenge on this walk was the crossing of the three-wire bridge over the torrential Water of Nevis at Steall. After this the knife edge of the Devil's Ridge leading to Sgurr a' Mhaim seemed like child's play.

Oliver was my companion on that occasion, and he was happy to finish there – that is, Sgurr a' Mhaim, not the three-wire bridge! – move his car to Polldubh and collect me after my descent from the Mullach.

It is possible to cover all the Mamores in a single, strenuous day, the choice of route being an interesting challenge in minimal repetition. However, this seems to do less than justice to such a magnificent range. Its splendours are best experienced through a variety of seasons, and the approaches from the south around Kinlochleven have a very different flavour from those which start in Glen Nevis.

The latter, of course, is breathtaking, with its waterfalls and ground level views of the elegant Mamores being particularly noteworthy and, with its range and diversity of interesting low-level walks, it will keep your non-climbing companions very fully occupied while you engage in higher things. And part of your reward will be the grandstand views of Ben Nevis and the Grey Corries northwards, and the Glen Coe peaks to the south.

<u>Sequence of Summits</u>	Meall Greigh, Schiehallion (2 Munros).
<u>Time of Year</u>	March.
<u>Start and Finish</u>	Loch Tay side; Schiehallion car park.

The process of rating oneself as a climber is one of continuous assessment. By now I rated myself as a two-Munro mam. That is to say, two separate mountains in the same outing came within reach. As an equivalent, if any walk required a descent to, say, 1,250′, the subsequent reascent was tantamount to starting again and could itself be considered a separate climb. The original excursion to the Lawers Group came close; this walk is an extreme example and is included for that reason only.

Meall Greigh remained from the first sortie and, from the Loch Tay side, could be no more than three hours' work – Pete's Rule applied to five horizontal miles on the map giving 2½ hours + the extra ½ hour required by Apocrypha 1. That would quite nicely take care of the morning. Hazel was despatched to explore Aberfeldy and timed her return to Lawers Village to perfection.

Nearby Schiehallion, not naturally combinable with anything else, would fill the afternoon, and so it did.

The advantage of this sort of doubling, apart from the two-for-the-price-of-one aspect, is that you need to carry provisions for only three hours. Back at the car you will replenish flasks, eat lunch and generally prepare for the next round. On this occasion the weather was kind and I remained dry all day.

The disadvantage is that there is a marked reluctance to get out of the car for the second ascent. Tired limbs are best kept moving!

Sequence of Summits	Ben Vane, Beinn Chabhair (2 Munros).
Time of Year	April.
Start and Finish	Glen Falloch.

And this is similar – here the two Munros were left over from other plans which never came to full fruition.

I have yet to experience good weather in the Arrochar Alps or to savour a view from one of their summits. I did once see the Cobbler and his wife from the train, many years ago. At the time of writing, Beinn Ime and, further to the north-west, Beinn Bhuidhe remain to be visited, so all is not yet lost.

My original plan for Ben Vane was to couple it with Ben Vorlich, approached from Ardlui station after having arrived there by train. The weather started foul and mostly stayed that way. At the summit of Ben Vorlich I realised that I had missed its North Top and had to back-track. The descent to the Loch Sloy dam had been difficult, and the decision to continue up Ben Vane was taken on the basis of a slight improvement in the conditions and a recalculation of the time required showing that I should just still be able to connect with the return train at Tarbet.

By the time I had reached the 2,100' shoulder north of the summit the weather had closed in again, the light was bad and it began to snow. I came down.

The four miles of road from the mouth of the Inveruglas Water to Tarbet was sheer hell. There is no pavement, the route is tortuous, it was dark and those in cars did not seem inclined to treat walkers in any way as bona fide road users.

By contrast Beinn Chabhair had been part of my original grand plan for a winter collection of 'The Crianlarich Five', on which the achievement fell magnificently short of the plan – a triumph of burgeoning experience over hope, one might say. On that walk I had had a discussion with someone going the other way in the fog on the ridge between Stob Garbh and Cruach Ardrain which led me to conclude that either he was going the wrong way or I was. In my then state of experience I naturally thought that, most likely, I was, so I came down. He was!

As an exercise try navigating in limited visibility from Cruach Ardrain's summit cairn to Beinn Tulaichean. No problems there, you might say, after due study of the map. If you can manage that, in such conditions you can almost certainly do anything else the Highlands have to offer.

'The Five' we reconstructed as a spring excursion to 'The Four', leaving Beinn Chabhair out on a limb, but slow going and failing light made it prudent also to defer An Caisteal, settle for 'The Three' and start the long haul back to the car at Inverlochlarig.

That left An Caisteal and Beinn Chabhair as a natural couple, best approached from the Glen Falloch direction. No problem there, you might agree. The weather was Arrochar Alpine. The wind was so strong that you would be blown across any flat stretches of ice, and never in a particularly convenient direction. Such conditions are energy sapping, and I decided to return from An Caisteal and save Beinn Chabhair, yet again, for another day.

On the descent I experienced quite dramatically that trick of the light which makes down look up in poor visibility. I had set the compass to take me into the flat upper reaches of Coire a' Chuilinn which would offer some respite from the wind, if not the raging sleet, rather than walk back over Stob Glas. As I came down out of the fog, which was clearing only slowly, the land below seemed to rise to the right and, as on all such occasions, the first reaction is – where've I gone wrong? and the second – where am I? On such occasions it is necessary, despite the weather, to stop and think – any sudden or panic reaction will probably be the wrong one. Down at the burn I made doubly sure that the water was flowing the way it should, for in that hilly country in mist it can be difficult to make any sense at all of the geography.

And so it was that Ben Vane and Beinn Chabhair came to be coupled – and as a two-Munro mam I knew I could do it. Ben Vane is a wee western terrier of a mountain. It just scrapes above the 3,000′ but packs a punch like no other. After it Beinn Chabhair was a long slog, the summit always seeming to be yet one more peak away. And on the way back, of course, I had my Alpine soaking!

Sequence of Summits   Carn Ghluasaid, Creag a'
                             Chaorainn, Sgurr nan Conbhairean,
                             Sail Chaorainn, Carn na Coire
                             Mheadhoin, Tigh Mor na Seilge,
                             Drochaid an Tuill Easaich
                             (3 Munros and 4 Tops).

Time of Year   April.

Start and Finish   Glen Cluanie.

The mountainous country to the north and south of the great
divide of Glen Cluanie and Glen Shiel is of outstanding beauty
and offers great scope for the planning of interesting, demanding
and varied outings. Here is one which, even although it fell
short of the original objectives, nevertheless proved a most
rewarding expedition offering some quite exceptional views. You
will no doubt wish to explore this fascinating area with walks
of your own design. There is plenty here for the low-level walker
also, including the famous through route to Shiel Bridge from
the east along Glen Affric.

This walk is basically straightforward with a well-defined path
leading to the first Munro and, thereafter, an exhilarating ridge
walk which, in its further reaches, offers splendid views back to
the northern corries of Sgurr nan Conbhairean and Carn Ghluasaid. This is just as well since the return journey starts as a
simple reversal of the outward. It was not necessary, however,
to reascend the Sgurr, as the traverse of its west face provided
a useful and effective alternative.

My plan had originally included the complete horseshoe of
A' Chralaig and Mullach Fraoch-choire as well. I had had them
constantly in view on the walk back and, therefore, had plenty
of time to consider the route at first hand. The immediate
concern was how best to include A' Chioch, which lies some

way off the main ridge. It is one of those flat-topped hills which tantalizingly challenges you to identify its summit unequivocally. There are usually parts which appear to be higher than the cairn. My preferred route would have involved a contour crossing of the Allt na Ciche from the Bealach Choire a' Chait but, even at that height, the bridge would have been a demanding exercise at that time of year.

The decision was forced by an obvious portent of a change in the weather, signalled, as is usual in those parts, from the west. The day had been a good one but one sensed that things were not going to last. A swift descent south down Meall Breac gave fast access back to the car. The first drops of soft, spring rain had already glistened the landscape. It had been a good day.

That whole massif is sufficiently complex and interesting not to yield its secrets fully to anyone in a hurry, wanting to finish the job in a single outing. It was good to have an opportunity to return, and I was certainly not disappointed.

| Sequence of Summits | Creag Pitridh, Geal Charn, Carn Dearg, Diollaid a' Chairn (3 Munros and 1 Top). |

| Time of Year | June. |

| Start and Finish | Loch Laggan. |

To the north-west and south-east of Loch Laggan there are great clusters of Munros where access is straightforward, if not exactly easy. In the summer, when daylight is plentiful, they can be assembled into substantial outings. Even Ben Alder himself is accessible from this direction, and with no greater inconvenience than from the more conventional starting points.

This is a walk which could have gone on for ever but for the appalling weather on the day. Of the three Munros perhaps Creag Pitridh is the most interesting. Its north-western face is a serious rock climb, not designed for mams or anybody else without proper equipment and experience.

I try to avoid going out and coming back by the same route, as I believe that you will rarely discover the innermost secrets of a mountain simply by going up and down by the easiest, or most direct, way. A circular journey taking in the main ridges, which will usually yield otherwise inaccessible views, is always a preferred option. The return, therefore, found me steaming, puffing and sweating round the west end of Beinn a' Chlachair, and heading north down the Allt Cam along a path which was boggy and eroded – not a pleasant walk.

There is a sense of isolation in this hinterland which is heightened by bad weather. You feel that the world must have ended without anyone letting you know. Thus it comes as a surprise to find other cars still on the road on rejoining a more ordered civilisation.

Sequence of Summits	Sron a' Choire, Puist Coire Ardair, Meall Coire Choille-rais, An Cearcallach, Creag Meagaidh, Stob Poite Coire Ardair, East Top, Sron Coire a' Chriochairein, Meall an-t-Snaim, Carn Liath, Stob Coire Dubh (3 Munros and 8 Tops).
Time of Year	June.
Start and Finish	Creag Meagaidh Nature Reserve car park.

Sherlock Holmes had one-pipe and two-pipe problems. I have one-dram and two-dram problems. How to do the whole Creag Meagaidh massif and return to the starting point was decidedly in the two-dram league! My solution was as given above. If yours is the same then take due care on the final descent. The route is criss-crossed with new deer fencing.

This was to be my 100th Munro, and I had chosen Creag Meagaidh as something special. Special indeed it is. A mountain for all seasons, it has everything. Grandeur, space, intimate corries, sheer cliffs, views north to the Corrieyairack Pass across the headwaters of the Spey and, on this occasion, weather to match after an uncertain start. This was compounded by the fact that the bridge across the Allt Coire Ardair to which M refers is fully described by Apocrypha 3!

The only thing against my suggested route is that it doesn't let you see into magnificent Coire Ardair from ground level. That walk, set against the varying back-drop of this wonderful range, I have made my archetypal Highland visit for those American guests who have only two hours or so to spare, but are prepared to put a bit of effort into finding out for themselves.

The walk into Coire Ardair – however far you want to go, and few give up on being told of the delights yet to come 'just round the next bend' – sufficiently encapsulates the Highland experience for those who have no more time, and it surely beats the video!

I have seen people grow in stature on this journey – they come to understand the limitations of their confinement. Men who rarely walk further than from their front door to their car door and whose golf is normally conducted from a buggy, experience at first hand and, probably, for the first time a radically different quality of life and, thereby, begin to understand 'Why do men climb mountains?' and a good many other things as well.

There is the added benefit of the deer park for those for whom even the mild ascent along a good path into the corrie is more than they feel they can manage.

Sequence of Summits	Sron na Lairige, Braeriach, Carn na Criche, Sgor an Lochain Uaine, Cairn Toul, Stob Coire an t-Saighdeir, The Devil's Point, Carn a' Mhaim (4 Munros and 4 Tops, or 5 and 3 based upon the 1997 Tables).
Time of Year	June.
Start and Finish	Coire Cas.

Although I have exalted Torridon, it would be invidious to single out that area as being in any way better than the Cairngorms. They are both very different and the experience offered by each is, of its type, exquisite. Although the Cairngorms could be said to be more touristy, offering, as they do, facilities which cater to a wide range of tastes, it is still possible to get away into the wilderness without undue delay. Indeed, it is the tourist facilities which bring the wilderness that much closer for, at this starting point, you are already over 2,000' without any expenditure of effort whatsoever. This makes the climbing of these relatively high peaks a less daunting task than might otherwise be the case.

There are many ways of dividing up this huge area into manageable walks, and many drams over many agreeable winter evenings were enjoyed in the preparation of an overall strategic plan. Needless to say, this never worked out in the field as the exigencies of the day made their decisive impact. Carn a' Mhaim fell by the wayside on the original Cairngorm Test and was tacked onto this walk almost as an afterthought.

This was the day of the Braemar to Aviemore run through the Lairig Ghru. That information was imparted by a runner who passed me on the summit of Braeriach and who had decided to do it the hard way and had time for no further conversation. The thought of running over Braeriach fills me with the same sort of awe as does the climbing of Mount Whitney in 4½ hours. The day being that of the run was confirmed by the myriad fresh indentations of running spikes in the soft mud when I was returning by the Lairig later in the afternoon.

It was about four in the afternoon as I sat by a waterfall somewhere on the south-west side of Ben Macdui, having decided not to return over the top. I would just tack on Lurcher's Crag on the return – another casualty of a previous journey. That moment was special. It had been a beautiful day, the water was delicious and the views across the great glacial divide were there to be savoured at length. I had completed the assignment and the whole world felt good. I leisurely picked a line which would take me down to the path through the Lairig with the least possible loss of height.

I have no idea to this day where the time went or why it took so long to cover the 2½ miles to the watershed, but by the time I was climbing out towards the Chalamain Gap all thoughts of Lurcher's had been firmly repositioned into the unspecified future.

Fortunately Hazel was away from home, so I was never called to account for my arrival back in Edinburgh in the wee small hours! The Cairngorms is big country.

Sequence of Summits	Mullach Coire nan Nead, Meall Glas Choire, Beinn Eibhinn, Aonach Beag, Geal Charn, Sgor Iutharn, Beinn a' Chlachair (4 Munros and 3 Tops).
Time of Year	July.
Start and Finish	Loch Laggan.

This was another monumental hike into the Ben Alder hinterland and one which offers splendid close-ups of that magnificent mountain. The cloud was up and down throughout the day, and the several dog-legs had to be negotiated with the greatest care. However, for an hour or so each side of midday things settled down, and we then had the benefit of the long views south-west down Loch Ossian and across to Rannoch Moor.

Andrew wanted to include Carn Dearg also on the return. I dissuaded him. It would have been consistent with the two-Munro ideal, but even in July the light doesn't last for ever. The descent from Beinn a' Chlachair turned out to be more difficult than we had expected – hauling tired bodies over awkward boulders – and the decision was probably a good one. If we had done it, we would probably have skipped Beinn a' Chlachair altogether.

The final mile or so was accompanied by a small band of sheep who had detached themselves from the main flock to pass various ribald comments upon our weird antics. They could not be persuaded to rejoin their colleagues and, in the end, we gave up trying.

Sequence of Summits	Am Faochagach, Cona' Mheall, Beinn Dearg, Meall nan Ceapraichean, Ceann Garbh (4 Munros and 1 Top).
Time of Year	July.
Start	Loch Glascarnoch.
Finish	Inverlael.

This is a superb walk, strenuous, exhilarating and demanding. The first challenge comes early: how to cross the Abhainn a' Gharbhrain. The second follows immediately: how to deal with the peat bog on its north-east side. The third is the stiff ascent of the east ridge of Cona' Mheall from Loch Prille. There is nothing which is particularly difficult, but care is required, especially on the steeper section of the last 200′ or so.

On this occasion the weather started mixed and gradually got worse. Thus the morning afforded some splendid views of the secret and spectacular country to the north, and just a glimpse of Meall nan Ceapraichean's south-east ridge before my starting up Beinn Dearg. After that, nothing. The fog closed in and the rain pounded.

My original plan had included Eididh nan Clach Geala, and the finding of the bealach linking this Munro to the Top of Ceann Garbh was a challenging navigational exercise given the near-zero visibility and the complexity of the terrain. Fortunately there are a number of wee lochans scattered about which offered a measure of positional confirmation. Even so, I was examining very carefully which way the water was flowing out of them to make doubly sure of my direction-finding.

At this stage I decided that Eididh could wait. There seemed little point in climbing it just to achieve a 'score' when it could be coupled with Seana Bhraigh for not much extra effort on a future visit to that beautiful place, when the weather, perhaps, would enable the scenery to be enjoyed to the full.

The rain duly hammered me all the way home but, in compensation, the waterfalls lower down the strath were truly magnificent.

Sequence of Summits	Carn Bhac, Carn Bhac – South-west Top, Beinn Iutharn Mhor, Beinn Iutharn Bheag, Mam nan Carn, Carn an Righ, Glas Tulaichean (4 Munros and 3 Tops).
Time of Year	August.
Start	Inverey.
Finish	Glen Lochsie.

I had had this walk buzzing round in my mind for over two years at least. Every time I looked at a map of the area the matter thrust itself forward. Not only did it need a friendly driver, but the best way to handle the giant zigzag in the middle never seemed quite clear cut. My answer is as given above, and I have no reason now to change it. Maybe your different approach will work as well.

The opportunity finally presented itself when Richard came to stay for a long weekend and was quite pleased at the thought of gaining another Munro. We would climb Carn Bhac together, and he would return to Inverey down the eponymous glen to play in Deeside until the time came to collect me over at Glen Shee.

This worked well. The early morning mist cleared by the time we had got up there, and I was able to direct him down his homeward route with a clear view of the way ahead. My own challenges were only just beginning. The steep ascent of Beinn Iutharn Mhor, after the long, boggy, undulating traverse from Carn Bhac, was energy sapping. The two Tops took their toll, and after the Mam there was the best part of 1,000' of ascent to gain Carn an Righ, still leaving Glas Tulaichean – hardly a pushover. I had seen it on a previous winter across the strath from Carn Bhinnein and knew exactly what I was in for!

Temptation began its corrosive undermining of the spirit. I could skip the Carn – it would always be there! Resist!! It was a lovely day, there was plenty of time left, no problems with food or drink, route finding straightforward – all I had to do was just put one foot in front of the other until finished. Easy really!

Richard was already at the Dalmunzie Hotel. He had fallen asleep in the car after his morning's exertions and Deeside remained unexplored.

Sequence of Summits   Sgurr an Fhuarail, Aonach
                       Meadhoin, Sgurr a' Bhealaich
                       Dheirg, Saileag
                       (3 Munros and 1 Top).

Time of Year   August.

Start   Cluanie Inn.

Finish   Glen Shiel.

Andrew and I had planned to walk from the Inn to Shiel
Bridge over the top, and including all the Sisters. How far the
achievement fell short of the plan!

The rain had been more or less horizontal, and the saddle
west of Saileag became the low point, both physically and
psychologically, of our journey. The corporate decision to descend was made purely by eye contact; words were superfluous
and probably wouldn't have been heard anyway. The Iberian
flavoured next port of call could wait for another day.

The descent down the sodden, steep, rank grass of the south
face and the soaking walk back to the car – five miles or more
– added their own dampness and gloom to a plan which, in
ideal conditions, would make a really good walk. Have a go!

I returned later to the Sisters, starting at the previous line of
descent. This time I made it west as far as Sgurr na Ciste
Duibhe before, yet again, giving in to them. Safe descents from
that ridge are not given away, and it is particularly important
to have well thought out fall-back options which can be invoked
in inclement weather or on those occasions when the flesh proves
weaker than the spirit. As I've indicated earlier, the Sisters are
difficult and demanding women. They crave your respect and
need to be approached in the right way!

I must also mention the most famous walk of all in this area:

the straight seven of the South Glen Shiel Ridge from Creag a' Mhaim to Creag nan Damh. By now you will not, of course, be surprised to hear that my original plan included the tacking on of Sgurr na Sgine, approached finally by its south-west ridge, and with an option on The Saddle as well!

Eight-thirty in the morning on the appointed day found me sitting in the car park of the Inn after driving up from Taynuilt, considering how best to recover from having brought the wrong OS sheet. It was raining stair-rods. A sketch map based on M's diagram would surely suffice. Just get up there to start with and then walk until the count reaches seven. There would certainly be a clear and unambiguous path on such a well-trodden ridge walk. Unfortunately it was not possible to see anything 'up there' above the cloud from which to derive any form of comfort.

When 11 a.m. arrived I convinced myself that the stair-rods were becoming less roddy. Just after 1 p.m. I found the summit of Creag a' Mhaim and, magic, the clouds were clinging to the north side of the ridge and I had a clear view not only to the next Munro, Druim Shionnach, but also to my left, south, all the way down into Glen Loyne. So, fully armed with compass bearings and with the next objective in sight, I boldly set forth.

Before the top of the Druim, however, the stair-rods had returned to impose a torture of pin pricks at that height, and all views had completely disappeared. M's diagram had shown the straightforward descents north from Maol Chinn-dearg; they would be my reserve escape if I decided to come down early. However, there was still plenty of time left to do the job, leaving Sgurr na Sgine for another day and perhaps, even, better weather. The Druim was number two, then three – Aonach air Chrith – and fourth, Maol Chinn-dearg. Navigation was blind but the path good.

I had had enough and decided to come down. Strange, the north ridge did not seem quite as user-friendly as my recollection of M's description of it would have had one believe. Perhaps you have already guessed why. There is a substantial bump between Druim Shionnach and Aonach air Chrith which I had counted as my number three. Thus I was descending from Aonach air Chrith itself, by a route which I wouldn't recommend to anyone.

Don't try and cut corners. You will be found out!

Sequence of Summits	Stob a' Choire Odhair, Aonach Eagach, Stob Ghabhar, Sron nan Giubhas, Sron a' Ghearrain, Stob a' Bhruaich Leith, Meall nan Eun, Stob Coir' an Albannaich (4 Munros and 4 Tops).
Time of Year	August.
Start and Finish	Victoria Lodge.

This is, of course, the east end of the earlier walk which started with Ben Starav. It was the one which Andrew and I considered doing in contrary motion but, on the day, discretion prevailed. Needless to say the weather began to improve very soon after we had made the decision, absolutely in accordance with Apocrypha 8.

We agreed to bypass Meall Odhar between Stob a' Bhruaich Leith and Meall nan Eun, and used its south face to descend to the bealach at the head of Coire nan Cmamh. It was a mistake. The route was an awkward, angled traverse over rocky ground and crossed many small ravines which slowed us down, and presented the danger of slipping in the wet unless great care was taken. These are not shown explicitly on the OS map. However, if you will perfect the art of inductive map-reading, you could reasonably predict that sort of terrain from the rock outcrop markings and the wiggles in the contour lines.

It is rarely self-evident whether it is better to go round something you don't need (or don't want) to climb, or to go over it. The best approach would seem to be to prepare for both and make a final decision on the day, allowing this to be conditioned by the usual factors such as weather, visibility, state of the ground, the existence of paths and the general difficulty of the terrain.

If you want a really good, long, hard, high-level summer walk, how about Stob a' Choire Odhair through to Ben Starav, taking in all the Munros and Tops along the way? I would be quite happy to have a go at this, but by the time I get back to it I shall probably be too decrepit for Munro climbing. I shall settle instead, before finally hanging up my boots, for the low-level route from Victoria Lodge through to Loch Etive down Glen Kinglass. This will be done on a sparkling day in deepest winter with the 'earth as hard as iron' to take best advantage of the special and spectacular scenery, provided I can get somebody to meet me in Ardmaddy Bay with a comfortable launch.

Sequence of Summits	Toll Creagach, Toll Creagach – West Top, Tom a' Choinich, Tom a' Choinich Beag, An Leth-chreag, Sron Garbh, Stob a' Choire Dhomhain, Carn Eighe, Mam Sodhail, Mullach Cadha Rainich, Sgurr na Lapaich (4 Munros and 7 Tops).
Time of Year	August.
Start and Finish	Glen Affric.

How best to walk all the high ground of that massif containing the highest points west of the Great Glen, bounded on the north by Beinn Fhionnlaidh and Toll Creagach, the west by Stob Coire Coulavie, the south by Creag Coire nan Each and the east by Toll Creagach, with the least number of repetitions, that is one of those two-dram problems which provides a good evening's entertainment during the long winter months.

This kind of planning invites a form of lateral thinking which detaches itself from a pure obsession with Munros and Tops – which, after all, are no more than a subjective and arbitrary definition of Scotland's high ground – and takes a wider and more comprehensive view of landscape and land-shape to evolve a rather different intimacy with it.

Indeed, there is no reason not to widen the scope of such an exercise to take in all the West Benula Forest and consider, for example, approaching the very remote Mullach na Dheiragain by boat along Loch Mullardoch. This adds its own dimension of interest and, at the same time, tackles the remoteness by using land-shape to best advantage.

The route documented here originally included the northerly ridge walk from Carn Eighe out to Beinn Fhionnlaidh and back (dropped on the day due to early slow progress in not very helpful weather), and early plans considered adding An Socach at the expense of some of the Tops of Mam Sodhail. There are many such possibilities.

I covered Beinn Fhionnlaidh and the two remaining Tops on a later visit and discovered a good path leading from near the col south-west of Mam Sodhail – the start of which is possibly going to be difficult to find in conditions of bad visibility – to the Beinn itself. I didn't follow it on the way out, as it appeared at first to drop too low, and preferred to find my own way. It was useful on the return, however, as it takes you below several rocky screes which lie on the more direct line of approach. All the way out and back there are quite splendid views of Mullach na Dheiragain and Sgurr nan Ceathreamhnan, and you can usefully spend some time considering how best to approach these two fascinating mountains, if you haven't already done so.

<u>Sequence of Summits</u>	Geal Charn, Meall Buidhe, Sgoran Dubh Mor, Sgor Gaoith, Carn Ban Mor, Meall Dubhag, Mullach Clach a' Bhlair, Tom Dubh, Monadh Mor, Beinn Bhrotain, Carn Cloich-mhuilinn (4 Munros and 7 Tops).
<u>Time of Year</u>	September.
<u>Start</u>	Glen Feshie.
<u>Finish</u>	Linn of Dee.

This was another epic Cairngorm hike, and one on which the weather at the start seemed unlikely to allow it to proceed to fulfilment. However, things steadily improved and the late summer sun beamed benignly from midday on.

For those of you doing Tops this was my answer to how best to include Tom Dubh. Although he is catalogued with Braeriach, my approach to that mountain would have involved coming all the way down and then reascending to The Angel's Peak. This had little appeal on the day. You might, of course, include him on a traverse from Braeriach to Mullach Clach a' Bhlair – I will leave that to you.

This walk offers splendid views of the interesting shape of Coire Garbhlach, but its general scale did not allow much time for side trips. And, of course, one must spare a thought for the great man himself when reaching the summit of Carn Cloich-mhuilinn.

At the end of a long day it was a great pleasure to be met by Hazel at the confluence of the Geldie Burn with the River Dee, and tell her all about it on the walk back to the car at the Linn.

<u>Sequence of Summits</u>	Meikle Pap, Cuidhe Crom, White Mounth – Creag a' Ghlas-uillt, Top of Eagle's Rock, Loch-nagar – Cac Carn Mor, Cac Carn Beag, Meall Coire na Saobhaidhe (1 Munro and 6 Tops).
<u>Time of Year</u>	September.
<u>Start and Finish</u>	Loch Muick.

This was conceived as a farewell to the White Mounth and included all those peaks not climbed in earlier excursions. Such a consummation is not always possible and depends on making and achieving good forward plans. So often one is left with a detached peak here and there at the extreme ends of a range and with no chance of combining them.

It was a holiday Monday which provided weather the best that late summer has to offer. I started early and the route was deserted, but by the time I had descended Meikle Pap and rejoined the main path, most of Aberdeen was out enjoying itself on the mountain. The White Mounth peaks, though, I had to myself.

Lochnagar is one of those occasional examples of a mountain having its twin peaks with their names the wrong way about. Perhaps this stems from the fact that either can look the taller, depending on the viewpoint. Or could it be that bulk rather than height was being taken into account?

The best part of Lochnagar is, of course, the northern corrie. This can be fully explored on the return from Meall Coire na Saobhaidhe. However, on this fine summer day my overwhelming recollection is the battering handed out by the insect hordes while coming round the north-east rump of Meikle Pap (if that is not a contradiction in terms), from which there was neither respite nor mercy. It is best not to dwell on such memories – otherwise you may never venture forth in the summer again.

| Sequence of Summits | Beinn a' Chreachain, Meall Buidhe, Beinn Achaladair, Beinn Achaladair – South Top, Beinn Mhanach, Beinn a' Chuirn (3 Munros and 3 Tops). |

| Time of Year | September. |

| Start and Finish | Achallader Farm. |

The first four peaks were left from an original winter walk starting with Beinn Dorain – the Beinn of the not-quite-reached summit. It had soon become clear that the original plan was far too ambitious in the prevailing conditions, and the descent into the chasm from the south-east tip of Beinn an Dothaidh had no appeal whatsoever on the day.

The coupling of Beinn Mhanach and its Top looked a good bet, and so it proved to be. Dominic was my willing dragoon on that occasion, and on the return leg we chatted our way quite happily well into Coire a' Ghabhalach until it finally dawned that all was not what it should have been. The col to Coire Daingean was above the cloud base, and we had chosen the wrong path after descending from Beinn a' Chuirn. A certain amount of back-tracking was now required and the compass – whose help, of course, should have been enlisted in the first place – used to confirm the required direction.

There is a perfectly good path all the way, and I'm not fully sure to this day how we managed to make such a dog's breakfast of finding it. Companionship adds a most welcome dimension to the mountain experience; it can also be quite distracting at vital moments.

Sequence of Summits	Stob a' Choire Mheadhoin, Stob Coire Easain, Stob Ban, Stob Choire Claurigh, Stob Coire na Ceannain (4 Munros and 1 Top).
Time of Year	May.
Start and Finish	Fersit.

My pre-antipodean ascent of Ben Nevis with Andrew had started and finished at the car park at the end of the road up Glen Nevis. The plan had been to do the Aonachs after the Carn Mor Dearg arête, but a physical and spiritual torpor had overpowered us – no doubt the side effect of dangling sore feet in a delicious mountain pool while soaking up the warm sunshine of a late spring day. Thank God for delicious mountain pools, provided precisely for this purpose!

Thus the walk sketched out above had strategic significance. If it was successful then the balance of the Grey Corries and the Aonachs could be cleared up with no greater effort on a later outing starting and finishing at Coirechoille. The key was to include Stob Choire Claurigh and the knife-edge traverse to Stob Coire na Ceannain on this first pass, and pick up Stob Coire na Gaibhre and Stob a' Choire Leith on the second. That would make the second an almost pure elliptical circuit, with just the side trip to Beinn na Socaich to dent its perfect symmetry.

The first pass worked well, but it required a supreme effort of will to climb Stob Choire Claurigh after the steep descent from Stob Ban. The second fell prey to Apocrypha 8. There had been unmitigated fog all the way to Stob Coire Easain, and I was not looking forward to the difficult and potentially dangerous navigation exercise which would link Sgurr Choinnich

Beag with Sgurr a' Bhuic – the key move in the whole strategy. So I left the rucksack at the top of Stob Coire Easain to go out and back over the Choinnichs, leaving the Aonachs for a return visit. Of course, by the time of my arrival at the westernmost point of the journey the cloud had lifted, the sky was azure and the views across to the Nevis Range just perfect. Such is life in the mountains! I even had to turn down the offer of a lift from Glen Nevis back to my car at Coirechoille from a fellow climber who evinced great sympathy with my frustrating predicament.

Although this second pass is a tall order, I am quite satisfied that it is achievable. The only unresearched bit is the descent east from Aonach Mor, and there appears to be nothing more than a steep, rocky ridge to start with. The final truth will be elucidated when I complete the Aonachs – now planned as a through walk from Glen Spean to Glen Nevis.

Sequence of Summits	Bynack Beg, Bynack More, A' Choinneach, Beinn Mheadhoin (Medwin!), Beinn Mheadhoin – South-west Top, Stacan Dubha, Stob Coire Etchachan, Sgurr an Lochan Uaine, Derry Cairngorm, Creagan a' Choire Etchachan (3 Munros and 7 Tops).
Time of Year	August.
Start and Finish	Coire na Ciste.

With the benefit of hindsight I would have taken the Tops of Beinn Mheadhoin in the order: Stob Coire Etchachan, South-west Top, Stacan Dubha. The descent from the former to the outfall of Loch Etchachan is over steep, rocky terrain and makes for extremely slow going – good ankle-spraining country. The route from Stacan Dubha, however, presents no such difficulty and, in retrospect, even looks shorter on the map. Why didn't I think of this at the time? Perhaps it was the thought of climbing back up onto the whale-back ridge of Beinn Mheadhoin itself that made the chosen route look better on paper. Paper in this case had involved one of my early experiences with the larger scale OS 1:25,000, and perhaps lack of familiarity with the medium also made its contribution.

This is the only time I have returned from an outing wishing I had planned it differently. By the time I had worked this out in the field, however, it was already too late to make the necessary revisions.

It was towards the end of this walk that I made a navigational error of monumental stupidity. The stretch from the top of Strath Nethy had taken longer than expected – it was difficult to resist continually turning round to see each new aspect of the inner Cairngorms as they disappeared from view – and as I began the climb out I was very conscious of needing to get a move on. The sun was low in the west and, as my return was now simply a matter of retracing the outward route and visibility was good, map and compass had been safely packed away. Surrounded by my hymenopteral halo, which I had long since given up trying to swat, I began the pull up the west bank.

This seemed to take much longer than I had remembered but, then, it had been a long day, and my speed would not have been fired by early morning vigour. At last the ridge and the descent towards the car. But no car. The sun was down below the horizon now, just a problem of not being able to see that far in the twilight. Hurry on, it'll soon come into view. But the land-fall to the north didn't look quite right. What's that deep trench? I don't remember that. Must be a trick of the light.

The brain is ever ready to rationalize, the much vaunted scientific approach too easily tossed aside. The truth stunned me: the sun hadn't been in the west at that time of year up there, it was in the north-west or even north of that. My line since leaving the strath had been 45° off course. Quick, out with the map while I could still see it.

The insect horde sensed the onset of panic and their attack became even more frenzied. Their target smelt of fear: move in for final victory.

I was over a mile away from where I should have been and just made it back to the car before the thickening twilight would have made further progress through the deep heather extremely difficult.

Never take anything as read in the mountains; they will always expose your weaknesses.

I marvel at the way insects are able to sense and take advantage of one's discomfort. On that occasion, once I was back on course and in control again, with the floods of panic finally

INSECTS ARE <u>USUALLY</u> ABLE TO SENSE AND

TAKE ADVANTAGE OF ONE'S DISCOMFORT

receding, they left me alone. Apparently miraculously, they just went about their other business.

This seems an appropriate point to dilate upon the matter of countering such aggression. Over time I have evolved these three strategies:

❊ Kill the ringleaders *pour encourager les autres*. This will have a cathartic effect on you and will offer only a short-term respite as the others regroup. I have never quite decided if the accompanying tribe is the same set of creatures following me all the way around a sixteen-mile circuit, or if a relief team moves in after the first mile or so to give the original crew a well-earned break, this in due course to be followed by further changes of personnel along the way. No biologist to whom I have spoken seems to know the answer, and all flies look the same to me.

After the declaration of war a warm truce can usually be agreed. You can sample from the chest down but keep away from my head. Violators will be summarily executed.

❊ Proceed waving a hankie above your head, changing it from hand to hand as each arm in turn becomes fatigued. This will have a significant effect on your balance and is, therefore, not recommended for knife-edge ridges or when rock-climbing is required. It is most useful during the long walk-out as it requires less effort than the first strategy, just a flick here and there rather than a major concentrated swat. At this stage in your journey the insects will be faster than you and less susceptible to that form of attack.

❊ The Greater Highland Midge cannot be dealt with satisfactorily by either of the above approaches as it doesn't seem to mind at which level it pitches its attack. Try a sprig of lavender or mint in your headgear; you should be able to convince yourself that it works and that the infestation would have been even more oppressive otherwise. Some recommend smearing raw garlic in the hair, a sort of repellent macassar! I've never quite been able to summon up the will to do this!

These aspects of entering into the harsh, raw world of nature can be highly amusing. Have you ever seen that contemptuous look on a sheep's face as you shamble past, dripping with sweat, breathless and showing signs of total exhaustion, which says 'And you think we're stupid!'?

Sequence of Summits   Beinn Bhreac, Beinn Bhreac –
                             West Top, Beinn a' Chaorainn,
                             Beinn a' Chaorainn Bheag,
                             Beinn a' Bhuird – North Top,
                             South Top
                             (3 Munros and 3 Tops).

Time of Year   August.

Start and Finish   Linn of Dee.

One of my original plans had been a walk starting at Coire na Ciste, finishing at Linn of Dee and taking in Bynack More, Beinn Mheadhoin, Beinn a' Chaorainn and Beinn Bhreac along the way – picking off the Cairngorms four Munros at a time. On the day transport arrangements did not allow the walk-through, and so this back-up plan was brought into action – hardly a lesser commitment.

I was glad of the good weather which accompanied me across the Moine Bhealaidh; this featureless, undulating plateau could well have been difficult to navigate in fog, although I guess that following a bearing of due north would have eventually yielded the right answer. Thereafter I could see from a distance the storms lashing the Dee Valley and managed to avoid most of them until the last twenty minutes of the return journey. So I enjoyed a dry day and a wet drive home and was now left with just the two further Tops of Beinn a' Bhuird and all of Ben Avon to be completed on a later outing, to round off that corner of the eastern Cairngorms.

Could I please appeal to any mams and anybody else using the Linn of Dee? There is a splendid car park, not shown on the OS 1:50,000 map, just 100 yards or so east along the road and lying to the north of it. In this you can secure your vehicle, and it will not obtrude on the beauty of the place. From the car park there is easy access to all northbound routes by a path also not shown on the map, and just the extra 100 yards back to the start of the westbound. If you use it, you will leave the Linn uncluttered with vehicles and so make it a much more pleasant place for residents and other visitors alike.

And while appealing could I also say a word to those of you (not mams, surely?) who leave our summits littered with beer cans, glass bottles (usually broken) and plastic detritus? Why do you do this? I don't understand you, this fouling of your own nest. In early climbs I would collect it up and dispose of it down below, but there was too much and the chore became impossible. Reluctantly, I now just leave it where it lies, an eyesore and a danger.

Sequence of Summits	Maoile Lunndaidh, Carn nam Fiaclan, Bidean an Eoin Deirg, Sgurr a' Chaorachain (2 Munros and 2 Tops).
Time of Year	September.
Start	Glen Strathfarrar.
Finish	Glen Carron.

The three glens which stretch westwards along near-parallel, latitudinal fault lines from Strathglass – Glen Affric, Glen Cannich and Glen Strathfarrar (why not just Glen Farrar or Strath Farrar?) – encompass some of our most beautiful countryside, and it is to these parts that I direct visitors who have no interest in climbing, don't want the West Coast and have limited time to spend in Scotland. They give a real flavour of what might have been, had the original forests been left intact. On a late summer afternoon the trees become almost incandescent in the setting sunbeams. Have a look at the off-the-beaten-track Plodda Falls, one of Scotland's best kept secrets, for an introduction to which I am greatly indebted to Douglas and Patricia, whose B&B close by is well worth using as a base from which to explore this beautiful hinterland. The falls are particularly exciting in winter.

This area offers scope for a variety of interesting outings, and the one I am describing is offered as a sample of many similar.

This splendid walk-through was planned to include Sgurr Choinnich, obviously, as well. However, by the time I had reached Sgurr a' Chaorachain it was clear that to visit the final Munro was going to put me over an hour late at my rendezvous with Hazel. As previously noted, it is important not to keep one's waiter waiting, much more so than to achieve the greatest possible score.

This was a super day with perfect weather and everything clearly visible. The view of Bidean an Eoin Deirg from the east end of Loch Monar was particularly memorable. It was the passage to this mountain from Carn nam Fiaclan which presented the major challenge of the day and which, no doubt, accounted for the whole journey taking longer than I had expected. There's one for you to work out for yourself if you ever pass that way.

For a long time I had intended Ben More on Mull to be my last Munro, its very singularity seeming to demand no less. In the event, that accolade went to Sgurr Choinnich. He had something to offer all the collected well-wishers who had tagged along for the occasion – an easy and pleasant walk-in, a superb riverside picnic spot for those not climbing, the excitement of the wire bridge, some optional rock scrambling for the hardier, the southerly views into some of the most secret parts of Scotland, a straightforward and not too arduous ascent – so it was quite clear that he never intended to be made part of this earlier outing. It was a great pleasure to return to that magical place for an event so momentous.

Sequence of Summits	Sgurr na Forcan, East Top, The Saddle, Trig Point, West Top, Spidean Dhomhuill Bhric, Sgurr Leac nan Each, North-west Top, Sgurr na Sgine (2 Munros and 7 Tops).
Time of Year	October.
Start and Finish	Glen Shiel.

This is not a long walk, and I have included it mainly to show a method of covering The Saddle and all its Tops, basically by going out from and back to the West Top along the main ridge. The walk is strenuous. From the West Top the return traverses to the Bealach Coire Mhalagain without the necessity of reascending the Munro. The lochan at the Bealach is a useful comfort in poor visibility, as navigation round the rotund southern spur of The Saddle needs due care lest you descend too far towards the south-west flowing Allt Coire Mhalagain.

If the Sgurr has no appeal at this point then it is easy to rejoin the route of ascent from here at the foot of the Forcan Ridge. This latter is the third most difficult thing you will climb on the mainland in your progress to mamhood, after Liathach's main ridge and the Aonach Eagach of Glen Coe. You can, therefore, measure yourself on it and get a feel for how you are likely to respond to these technically more demanding climbs.

The descent from Sgurr na Sgine was down the north-east prow of Faochag (worth doing in its own right) of which there is a most impressive view below from the valley floor of Glen Shiel.

So now you have the full story – or nearly so. Here are three further combinations of two which I have not discussed in detail:

Stuchd an Lochain with Meall Buidhe, both the greater and lesser Buachaille (now offering four-for-the-price-of-two!) and Sgor na h-Ulaidh with Beinn Fhionnlaidh, all of which come under the two-Munro general umbrella but may not at first sight suggest themselves as natural pairs.

The 27 walks I have described include 94 Munros and 93 Tops (95 and 92 based upon the 1997 Tables) and cover over one third of the total task. Some of them can be regarded as representative. They are similar to others in the same general area, and it seemed unnecessary to document all of them comprehensively here.

I have been at pains to confess the failures (if such a word is appropriate in this context) as well as the successes. I have even noted the occasional near-disaster.

I hope you will draw strength from this mixed catalogue of experience, not so much to follow in my footsteps either physically or metaphorically, but to have before you an example of what's possible, upon which to build your own personal and unique plan of campaign, fully tuned to your own aspirations and capabilities. You will surely learn something new about yourself, or at least remember something you'd forgotten. You will also come to understand John Steinbeck's meaning when he wrote, 'A journey is a person in itself, no two are alike, and all plans, safeguards, policies and coercion are fruitless. We find after years of struggle that we do not take a trip; a trip takes us.'

Climbing a mountain is a simple metaphor for life's rich passage. We arrive at the start; we are brought up; we gain experience; we stumble and fall; we have limited vision; we make mistakes; we enjoy successes; we are elated and disappointed; we reach a peak; we decline; we return whence we came. Or is this making a mountain out of a metaphor?

I wish you the best of luck with your own personal journey!

CHAPTER XV

Endgame

At about the time I was down to my last fifty there dawned a conflict of expectation. On the one hand, the numbers suggested that one was nearing the home straight. On the other, there were some far-flung westerly peaks yet to be attempted, as well as Mull and Skye. It soon became clear that the time and effort which would be required to finish the challenge were not going to be represented accurately by the simple arithmetical proportion of number remaining to overall total.

I had not intended to leave Skye until so late in the project. Slender opportunities for making the required time available came and went, and in the end I put it in the diary just as if it were a future business appointment. More is written about climbing in Skye than in any other part of Scotland. Much of it is contradictory. This is my attempt to make sense of it: not the blue-sky Skye of the postcards but Skye as it really is.

You will know that the Cuillin are different from the mainland mountains. How different you will discover during your exploratory attempt. My first recommendation, therefore, is to spread Skye over several extended visits (at least three) and use the first one to measure your own capabilities against those mighty mountains. On the second you can then plan to do those climbs which you are happy doing without assistance and on the third bring in the hired help for the rest. If you are one to whom Skye is addictive then you will want to return as often as possible and will not be concerned with squeezing the last possible drop of available adventure from each visit. If not, then you will want to plan your visits for optimum achievement. My other recommendations are embedded in the following:

❊ Skye is very wet. All the approach paths are eroded and boggy. The use of 4WD fun-vehicles hasn't helped. You will climb Skye with wet feet.

❊ Skye is very cloudy. Statistically you will get a view from the top one day in six. This may not last for long. Enjoy it while you can.

❊ Skye is very rough. After your first day your fingertips will be so sore that when you wash your face your chin will feel rougher than gabbro. On subsequent days you will evolve scrambling techniques that require minimum use of the hands!

❊ Skye is very busy in summer. You may have to queue to get on the Inaccessible Pinnacle.

❊ Skye is educational. The mainland will never be quite the same again. Your performance and capabilities will improve beyond measure. The Hunter's Pass on Ben Attow's spiny west ridge or the Ceum Grannda of Beinn Eighe, for example, will seem as nothing after the Cuillin corries.

❊ Skye is breathtakingly beautiful. Its unique combination of ragged ridges, panoramic views, compactness, serene seascapes and clouds in formation will form a cradle of memories which will never leave you. In short, Skyescapes are superlative.

❊ Skye is slow. Abandon all Pete's rules. You will manage about one third to one half of what you might achieve on the mainland. This is partly due, of course, to your wishing to savour the experience to the full.

❊ Don't abandon your compass. Although Sgurr na Banachdich confuses it, I have found it otherwise reliable and effective. However, be duly circumspect.

✳ Don't abandon those principles of route planning which allow you to find your own way. This is always much more satisfying. For example, I found the flat, c. 35°, south-west face of Sgurr nan Eag a straightforward if strenuous way to the summit (about four hours from Glen Brittle in bad weather and poor visibility), and an approach to Sgurr na Banachdich up Coir' an Eich worked well (2½ hours on a perfect day), and is, possibly, the only really hill-walker-friendly means of addressing that magnificent mountain. Neither of these routes have I seen recommended, although the latter is obviously well-trod.

The problem on Skye is not the Inaccessible Pinnacle, the incredible experience of climbing which utterly surpasses the hill-walker's vocabulary for describing it. You know that that is the most difficult Munro and will plan and provision accordingly, commanding whatever assistance you need. The problem is how best to tackle the main ridge.

If you are competent with ropes you will manage all the difficult bits satisfactorily. If, like me, you prefer to travel light then you will need to divide the ridge into segments bounded by known discontinuities such as the TD gap or the south wall of Sgurr Mhic Choinnich. These segments will then become your foundations for route planning.

If, also like me, you grapple from time to time with residual vertigo then you may wish to be on the main ridge for as short a time as possible. In this case the routes recommended in M will be particularly useful. It was at such a time that I made the decision to relegate the Skye Tops down my list of priorities and concentrate single-mindedly on the Munros alone. I was exploring around the summit of Sgurr na Banachdich, considering for half an hour or so the splendid but terrifying orthogonal symmetry of Sgurr Thormaid and how best to respond to its challenge to have a go, finally deciding that that was one on which I was going to need some support. And the Bhasteir

Pinnacle of achievement – the author, Andrew and friends on the
most difficult Munro.

Tooth's worse! Ah well, it's useful to leave something still to be achieved, otherwise life would have less purpose! Following the 1997 revisions to the Tables, I must surely return to the new Top of Knight's Peak, which also looks as if climbing it may require some support.

And there is the admission that the phobia was never completely overcome. All I had succeeded in doing was to command sufficient control of mind over matter occasionally to mitigate its effect when called upon to do so. From Skye came the final lesson that self-control is arbitrary, difficult and incomplete. How we men and women delude ourselves otherwise!

One quite extraordinary Skye experience worth recording was being caught on a ledge of the steep headwall of Coir' a' Ghrunnda in the down draught of a mountain rescue helicopter, which seemed to be trying to blow me off in order to drum up some extra business. I discovered later that it had returned to collect one of its own team from above who preferred not to descend the hard way, during which process I could clearly see its rotors, but the body was just out of sight over my horizon, perhaps 50' above me. It was a frightening experience as I clung for dear life to a rock while the helicopter completed its manoeuvre. Big boys' toys ...

You may be interested at this point in the year-by-year progress towards mamhood, which, in my case, looks like this -

At end of year	Munros climbed	Target	Tops climbed
I	82	75	51
2	157	150	115
3	213	200	180
4	231	250	199
5	260	277	220
6	273	277	230
7	277	277	235

spread over a total of 143 climbing days. These numbers are based on the 1990 Tables. However, since I had included the Tops in my challenge (and all the 'new' Munros were previously in that category, with none on Skye), I was already in conformance with the 1997 standard. No doubt many current munroists are now engaged in the process of cleaning up their boots in preparation for yet one further push!

The figures and targets are cumulative. Those for year 1 collect together everything which had been climbed before the real campaign began and, therefore, do not represent a true year's work. The first target was originally set conservatively at 50, as I had no idea at that early stage of the adventure of any more realistic number. Once passed, I revised it up to 75!

In the fourth year, beyond the 200 mark, as already noted, I had underestimated the time required to finish the job, given that most of what remained would not allow the great collections of four and five in an outing to be sustained. I was now down, almost, to a single Munro here and a Top there, all the odd bits and pieces that had not been previously included, or which had been dropped from original plans as fall-back procedures were called into play. This was in spite of deliberately leaving some hills near Edinburgh right to the last minute so that the final laps were not confined exclusively to the islands and far North-west, and there was still something local to do on a fine, crisp and sparkling winter's day. It is at this time that your resolve will need to be strengthened, and any temptation to slow down resisted. You could, of course, spread the task over more years, but will the determination and fitness hold out . . .?

It was now that I developed the notion of the three- and four-day spring, summer and autumn event. On the first day, I would plan to arrive at the start of a six- or seven-hour climb at lunch-time and arrange some overnight accommodation in a more or less friendly B&B. Day two (and three of a four-day event) would be committed to a ten- or twelve-hour journey after negotiating an earlier than usual breakfast with the more or less compliant landlady. The final day would then involve a shorter route in the morning, followed by an afternoon or evening return home at a reasonable hour. This offered a good balance between travel and climbing time and ensured that the endgame did not become excessively prolonged.

In the summer, of course, most mainland Munros are possible in a day trip from Edinburgh if you set off early enough, but the remoter ones would hardly be a pleasure on that basis.

In doing all this I have counted myself lucky in a number of ways.

First, in running my own business I have not been dependent on the goodwill of an employer for time off. When things have been quiet in the office, I have been able to leave matters in the hands of trusted others and slip away unnoticed for a day or two. Thus I have not been confined to weekends and public holidays and have been able to avoid some of the worst of crowded roads and ridges. I have even managed to slip in a few sorties on business trips when, for example, a meeting in Glasgow ending earlier than expected left the Arrochar Alps accessible on a weekday afternoon.

Secondly, I have had a willing wife, not just to fetch and carry, but to be there at the end of the day providing monumental assistance in getting me dry, sore feet tended, dealing with all aspects of victualling and, generally, turning me round ready for the next day's exertions. I can say with total confidence that, had it not been for Hazel's complete support, this whole project would not have been possible.

Thirdly, I owe a debt to Andrew, my willing Sherpa in the days before he discovered drink and women. His carrying of loads heavier than I would have wished to bear and his idiosyncratic planning of those trips whose routes I entrusted to his design, all added to the variety and spice of what started as a joint ambition and which, I have no doubt, he will achieve in due course in his own time. Already he is a more competent hard rock man than I shall ever be, and I was particularly grateful for his chumming me round the more difficult parts of Skye and applying a strategic push or pull at certain crucial moments.

So that's the project done: seven years of intermittent concentrated bursts mixed in with all the other demands on one's time. It has covered all the mainland Munros and Tops, all the Skye Munros and about half its Tops, and Ben More on Mull, the climbing of the latter proving an interesting exercise in the effective use of integrated public transport. There remain the memories, the experiences and, above all, the people. It has been a life-enriching adventure I wouldn't have missed for anything! If you take it on, there are certain to be times of doubt and difficulty. Is it actually within your capabilities? Can you afford the time? Will you take the risk? What about other important priorities? Your resolve will be put seriously to the test. Resist! You too can do it! And if you want to achieve a world first also, how about doing them in alphabetical order, everything from A' Bhuidheanach Bheag to West Meur Gorm Craig? Now there's a challenge!

In alphabetical order here are the six Munros which I regard as the most remote and difficult to access (but not necessarily the most difficult technically) – A' Mhaighdean, Ladhar Bheinn, Lurg Mhor, Mullach na Dheiragain, Seana Bhraigh and Sgurr Dubh Mor. Small rock samples from the summits of each now adorn my office, lest I forget and others disbelieve. From Ladhar Bheinn I took one from each of its twin peaks, just in case!

CHAPTER XVI

Apocrypha

I will finish with some not entirely tongue-in-cheek rules and guidelines which may be applied to our calling, and about which other authors seem curiously reticent. Here is the inside story! Perhaps things work out better for them! Perhaps, even, they will work out better for you!

1. No matter how careful your planning or precisely calculated your journey time, you will arrive back at base at least half an hour later than you estimated.

2. This is still true even if you add an extra half-hour in an attempt to thwart it.

3. Be prepared to discover that well-documented river crossings are no more than a figment of someone's imagination.

4. Forest fire breaks are never aligned in your direction of travel.

5. You will invariably carry a spare pair of bootlaces but will not, in fact, be able to locate them on those rare occasions when the wet acid peat has rotted that one which seemed so strong earlier in the day.

6. The 10p coin which you habitually carry for emergency

phone calls will have disappeared through an unknown hole in your pocket on the very day that you first need to use it.

7. Anything you accidentally drop (lunch wrapper, map, compass, balaclava, glove) will be wind-blown or will bounce in such a way as to make its retrieval a life-threatening exercise.

8. If you make a decision during an outing which depends upon the weather continuing to do a particular thing, or to change from doing a particular thing, then the weather will do exactly the opposite just after you have reached a point at which your decision is then irreversible.

9. If your own innate and infallible sense of direction tells you different from your compass then your own innate and infallible sense of direction is invariably wrong.

10. You will have this lesson brought home several times on your progress to mamhood, and will only finally accept its truth quite late on in your achievement. As a result you will have explored parts of Scotland which were never in your original plans.

11. If you are troubled by a stone in your boot then remove it immediately. Otherwise, you will always be tempted to look for a more convenient place to stop, a dry rock to sit on for example, and in the looking will wriggle your toes from time to time to try and dislodge the irritant to a more comfortable position. By the time you have achieved this, you will be near enough to the end of your journey to convince yourself that it is hardly worthwhile stopping anyway.

12. Within ten paces of having removed the boot, emptied out the stone and other sundry debris and replaced the boot, you will discover yet another stone.

13. You will now find that the replaced boot is much tighter than its partner and thus remind yourself of why you preferred to leave the original stone undisturbed in the first place.

14. Do not set your map and compass on the roof of the car, for the mountain you are looking at will not be in the place indicated. In general, if you think your bearing may have been affected by extraneous magnetic sources (iron posts or galvanized boulders, for example) then take several readings within a line or square of around twenty yards. If they are consistent, they will almost certainly be accurate.

15. If you need to remove your gloves for any reason, do be sure to put them back on again. Otherwise, when you return to where you thought you left them, it will prove to be not where you left them.

There is one small matter outstanding. I climbed Ben Vorlich (Perthshire) just two days before my fiftieth birthday. To qualify absolutely for mamhood I really ought to do it again. I plan to do this with James so that my last over fifty as his grandfather will be his first. This not only appeals to my sense of symmetry, but will pass the Munro baton firmly down two generations for whatever he may choose to do with it. Could this be the start of a dynastic tradition? However, I do hope that none will feel any more than a personal compulsion to take it on, for the sheer joy of doing it rather than any pressure to conform.

Finally, what next? Some suggest the Corbetts. I have no doubt I could do them, but must now downgrade mountain climbing in my list of priorities. The Corbetts, of course, will take you to parts of Scotland void of Munros. Ardgour, most of the islands and the far North are prime examples. One can visit these places, anyway. However, I am very conscious of the quiet and uncomplaining support given by Hazel most of all, and the things which she has been denied, her pleasures and goals, while I have pursued mine.

I shall always climb, to keep fit, as long as I am fit to continue. The hills of Sutherland, in particular, beckon, as well as many in other parts of the world. Beinn Dearg of beloved Torridon is a must – the highest mountain in Scotland not a Munro. Can it really be lower than Beinn a' Chlaidheimh? Beinn Damh also looks good for a day's exhilaration and might even be fun in Torridontal rain! Sgurr a' Choire-beith at Barrisdale also entices, and climbing it could be a useful pre-emptive move against any future promotion to Munro status in some post-millennial revision of the Tables. However, these will be done casually and mixed with other pleasures. No more annual objectives. No more pins in maps.

I would love to climb Stac Pollaidh. It is unique in Britain, a rare singularity, the nearest thing to an Arizonan butte. All I know who have walked its ramparts tell of the grotesque erosion, much of which is visible from the roadside. I have no answer to this and am conscious of having added the weight of my own footfall to the total sum of wear and tear in our landscape.

Could we who love the wilderness and derive such special satisfaction from it not agree to abstain from this wonderful mountain so as not to destroy it further? Could we treat it as in some sense sacred, our own Uluru, to be admired but never again touched? Is this too fanciful or too much to give up? I leave you with that thought – until the next ice age.

Explanations of Terms which may be Unfamiliar to the General Reader

Arête	A sharp, steep-sided ridge connecting two peaks.
Barffing	American word meaning vomiting.
Bauchles	In English, slippers, hence comfortable, homely things.
Bealach	Gaelic word meaning mountain pass.
Bevvying	The heavy drinking of alcoholic substances.
Bivvy bag	From bivouac: an overnight (usually) resting place on a mountain, not involving the use of a tent. A specialized sleeping bag to make this warmer, safer and more comfortable.
Bothy	A man-made, permanent mountain refuge.
Breeks	In English, trousers.
Burn	In English, stream, i.e. small river.
Cleg	Nearest English equivalent: horse-fly.
Col	The low point on a ridge connecting two peaks. Used more or less synonymously with bealach (q.v.).
Corbett	A Scottish mountain of 2,500′ or over which is not a Munro or Top (q.v.). The Corbetts are more precisely defined than Munros in terms of required horizontal distance and vertical fall

between any two of them. However, collectively they represent no more than yet another arbitrary subset of Scotland's high ground.

Cornice An overhanging band of compacted snow attached to a mountain ridge but not supported by any solid ground. Cornices build up in winter and are dangerous things to be on, particularly if the land-fall is steep.

Corrie The hollow part of a mountain between two ridges. It is often convenient to distinguish between the upper (or inner) corrie, giving onto the summit ridge, possibly, and the lower (or outer) corrie, further down the hill and, perhaps, wooded.

Crampon A metal attachment, fixed to the base of a boot, which has protruding spikes in various forms to assist grip when climbing on ice.

Deleted Top A Top (q.v.) that was in Munro's Tables (q.v.) but has been removed in a later revision.

Escarpment The steep terrain between sudden changes in horizontal level; a cliff, for example.

Gabbro Hard, rough, granite-like rock which is characteristic of Skye.

GPS Global Positioning System. An arrangement whereby information transmitted from satellites is analysed by a hand-held computer to give its user his position anywhere on earth.

Lochan A wee loch. In English, a small lake.

Lorimer Sir Robert Stoddart Lorimer: a well kent (q.v.) Scottish architect of the late nineteenth/early twentieth century who built castles in the air, amongst other things.

BUILT CASTLES IN THE AIR

Muckle	In English, large.
Munro	A Scottish mountain of 3,000′ or more in height. Named after Sir Hugh Thomas Munro, who first catalogued and documented them in the late nineteenth century. His relatively primitive surveying equipment led to some (but surprisingly few) errors. The metrication of the Ordnance Survey gave rise to further revision. Thus there is a web of controversy surrounding the whole matter. Should the Munros be as Sir Hugh left them or true to their definition? Furthermore, he specified no criteria by which distinct mountains should be separated. He identified main peaks (the Munros) and subsidiary peaks belonging to the same mountain but themselves over 3,000′ (the Tops). One must not lose sight of the fact that all such analysis is arbitrary; one may, therefore, take from it only what one needs.
	I am avoiding any further discussion of Munro, his times, his motivation and his ideals, and the validity of the whole process of the orderly classification of disorder, with the excuse that these are covered by other authors to a much higher standard than I could manage. For the general reader the accounts in M and the Tables (q.v.) may well suffice.
Munro's Tables	(The Tables). Lists of the Munros (q.v.) divided into convenient geographical sections, giving map references and heights of each. The point of reference for this book is the 1990 edition.
Munroist	One who has climbed the Munros (q.v.).
Oxters	In English, armpits.

Radio token	A device for controlling the entry of trains into single-line stretches of track so that they are in no danger of collision.
Recce	Short for reconnaissance, i.e. a preliminary excursion to plan the best route.
Saddle	Synonymous with col (q.v.), which has this shape.
Scaffing	In English, scuffing, in the sense of scratching or roughening.
Scree	A run of loose, small rocks and stones on a mountain slope.
Sheep fank	Pen for corralling the said animals.
Strath	In English, valley, but with the further connotation of its being wide and flat.
Tables	See Munro's Tables.
Top	A Scottish peak of 3,000′ or more, but lower than a taller mountain of which it may be considered to form part.
Well kent	In English, well known.

Index of Mountains and Other Places